INDEPENDENCE DAY

INDEPENDENCE DAY

*What I've Learned About
Retirement from Some Who've
Done It and Some Who Never Will*

STEVE LOPEZ

HARPER HORIZON

Published by Harper Horizon, an imprint of HarperCollins Focus LLC.

Any internet addresses, phone numbers, or company or product information printed in this book are offered as a resource and are not intended in any way to be or to imply an endorsement by Harper Horizon, nor does Harper Horizon vouch for the existence, content, or services of these sites, phone numbers, companies, or products beyond the life of this book.

ISBN 978-0-7852-8873-2 (Ebook)
ISBN 978-0-7852-8872-5 (HC)
ISBN 978-0-7852-9011-7 (SC)

Library of Congress Control Number: 2022931407

Printed in the United States of America
23 24 25 26 27 LBC 5 4 3 2 1

For Jeff.

There he is, coming through the door,

filling up the room.

"As you get older, you become the person you always should have been."

—David Bowie

CONTENTS

INDEPENDENCE DAY

ONE

IT'S THE FOURTH OF JULY AND I'M LOUNGING IN MY BACKYARD, thinking about a different kind of Independence Day. The day I say goodbye to work as I know it. I live at the top of a hill, and on a clear day, I can see Santa Monica Bay twenty miles away. But the view to the west is a little hazy at the moment, just like my thoughts about when to walk away. Some days I know I'm ready. Other days I fear I'd be lost. I left college on a Tuesday night in 1975, started work the next morning, and I haven't stopped. It's all I know and, what's more important, it's a big part of who I am.

My wife, Alison, a freelance writer who is seven years younger than I, has just come out of the house. She beat me badly at tennis this morning. A lean, lithe youngster taking full advantage of a hobbled graybeard with two fake knees and a pacemaker. That's my excuse, at least. She saunters over and takes a look at our bamboo sofa and asks if I think we should get rid of it and buy teak furniture instead. This is not a difficult question for me. I am not the kind of person who takes a gander at a perfectly serviceable lounge or a kitchen table or a refrigerator and wonders, on a whim, if it's time to spend good money to replace it. But that's not an argument worth having, so I point out to Alison that the bamboo is all-weather and low maintenance. The latter feature appeals to me more than ever, because I can think of far better things to do with a weekend than sand and varnish furniture. Alison nods and goes back inside the house.

The house is not huge, and that's another consideration. We each like our space, and as a freelance writer, Alison's office is our house. But when the pandemic hit, and I was forced to work from home much more than usual after my office was closed for safety reasons, we bumped into each other now and then. It felt like a preview, a test of whether either of us can handle the closeness my retirement will bring. Alison would see me planted in the den, which is mere feet from her office, and ask, "Are you going to be in this room much longer?" God willing. Ten years. Twenty. I'm not sure how much time I have left.

Fireworks explode in every direction around me, even though there's plenty of sunlight left in the day. It's been like this since Memorial Day, partly because nearly everyone in Los Angeles is a pyromaniac at this time of year. If another country invades the United States right now, we're ready in L.A. We will blow any landing infantry or enemy air force to kingdom come with torpedo-sized bottle rockets, military-style M80s, and Roman candles. We are armed to the teeth this year, because people have time on their hands and are hungry for some cheap do-it-yourself entertainment, partly because sanctioned fireworks displays have been canceled. On the news last night, I watched a house not far from ours burn to the ground because some knuckleheaded amateur sparked a blaze. You never know what's coming at you next.

The symphony of pyrotechnic percussion makes me worry about our daughter, Caroline, who is out at the moment—safely distancing, she assures us—because she is going stir crazy. Pandemics, lockdowns, teenagers. Bad combination. I didn't see her leave the house today, but I seldom do, because her departures are like prison breaks. I don't hear a sound, but I peer through the front window and see the car is gone. She's had days where she sleeps late, wakes up mummified, and doesn't communicate until the evening rolls around. Then, when Alison and I are exhausted, she won't stop talking. God, I love her, and I'm going to be in tears the day she leaves. Last year at this time we were on vacation in Italy. I wanted to take that trip because I know we are running out of time. It can't be much longer before Caroline tells us she'd rather start an ant farm or do dishes than go on vacation with us. We're still good for the occasional family day trips, and we're usually on a beach when school lets out and our work and school schedules free up a bit. But I'm playing it safe. When the pandemic was in full force, half the deaths from COVID-19 were in my age group. If I'm not burned alive by errant fireworks, it'll be the virus that gets me. Maybe I should just retire today.

Speaking of Caroline, there's a letter on our kitchen table from the women's tennis coach at Occidental College. He's interested in her as a possible recruit. This would be the perfect school for Caroline in many ways. Occidental has a pretty, tree-shaded, midsize campus and it's a solid liberal arts school. Years ago, a freshman named Barack Obama was a student there. But Occidental has one major strike against it. It is roughly two miles from our house. If Occidental were to offer my daughter a full scholarship, she would probably decline and set her sights on one of the many American schools that think it's okay to charge working people $75,000 a year. My retirement hinges in part on that decision and how much it's going to cost. But I can guarantee you, especially after four months of forced family closeness, that Caroline is going to put more than two miles of distance between us.

I'm not complaining about any of this, by the way. Life is better than good, all things considered. But it's time to begin sorting things out, to the extent that's possible in the midst of strong evidence that the world is about to end. I know people my age who have already retired, couldn't wait to sign off, and never looked back. And among colleagues my age who are still working, one of our frequent topics of conversation is when to go. I'm not usually one for making pro-con lists, because I tend to trust my gut more than my head. But maybe I should give it a try.

Okay, three good reasons to pull the plug now rather than hang on longer.

Number One: I've been working full-time for forty-five years and will be almost sixty-eight at this time next year. In my parents' generation, people had the good sense to go for full-time leisure at sixty-five or earlier, before they needed hearing aids, before their toenails turned yellow, and before they considered buying one of those bathtubs you enter through a door before turning on the water, so you don't have to face the impossible feat of scaling the fourteen-inch wall of a standard tub.

Number Two: I'd still be young enough to do things, go places, maybe surprise myself with new interests. I like to cook, but because of my work schedule, I don't have time for formal cooking classes. Spanish classes would be nice or maybe a temporary move to, say, Barcelona, so I could finally get fluent, like my dad, the son of immigrants from Spain. Or maybe I could move to Sicily, where my maternal grandmother is from and where some towns have been offering homes for sale at a dollar each. Yes, a dollar for a house, more or less, if you agree to do some maintenance and restoration. It's seen as a way to revive dying economies in towns decimated by a population exodus. Why would I pass up a chance to take leisurely swims in the island's postcard-perfect lagoons, grow plump tomatoes in my garden, sip wine from local vineyards, and watch the sun set over the Mediterranean? If I wait too long to retire, I may not be healthy enough to do any of that.

Number Three: No more deadlines. I'm in my fifth decade of being ruled by deadlines, which requires constant vigilance. Sometimes I'm awakened in the middle of the night by a hungry beast that has to be fed constantly. What's the next column? Do I have any decent ideas? When's the last time I really knocked one out of the park? I lie there, wondering if the mayor needs a good flogging or if there's something clever that I haven't already said about pitchfork militants who refuse to wear masks because it infringes on their constitutional rights. In my job, you have to produce without excuse. It's not like fishing, where you can go out on a boat, come back, and say you didn't catch anything today. The editor always wants to know what you've got coming. And speaking of fishing and going out on boats, I might just spend my first month of retirement doing nothing else.

Okay, not bad. Now let's see if I can come up with three good reasons *not* to retire.

Number One: My retirement fund has taken a beating during the pandemic, and I need time to build it back up. What timing, by the way. Just as I'm ready to get out of class and go to recess, a killer bug stalks everyone on the planet. And the global economy collapses. And traveling anywhere is a game of Russian roulette. That had to happen now? I'm reminded of the movie *Lost in America*, where Albert Brooks says screw it all, retires, buys a motor home, and hits the open road. He makes his first stop in Vegas, where, while he's asleep, his wife loses their entire nest egg in one bad streak at the craps table. Penniless, Brooks ends up so desperate he takes a job as a crossing guard.[1] My 401(k) has recovered a good bit since the low point during the pandemic, but let's face it, this virus could easily be followed by another that leads to an even greater global collapse, and I don't think I'd make a very good crossing guard.

Number Two: This is related to Number One. I work in an industry that has lost tens of thousands of jobs. Newspapers by the dozens have folded, and I'm lucky to still be on a payroll, so why not keep cashing checks until the lights go out? I've got a pretty good résumé, but if I hang it up a year from now, and Alison dumps the entire nest egg at a craps table, I may not be able to find work again. As the industry tanks, editors are not putting job applications from sixty-eight-year-olds at the top of the pile.

Number Three: I'm a soldier in the fight against age discrimination, which is running amok in the economy and the entire culture. Bodies have been piling up in nursing homes, where testing for COVID-19 hasn't even been required, and nobody seems to care all that much. They're just old people, right? In my own newsroom, there's been a youth movement for many years now, which is as it should be. The business needs fresh blood, new ideas, different perspectives. But the strongest newsrooms are those in which a healthy mix of youth, experience, and talent blend seamlessly and journalists learn from each other, challenge each other, and elevate each other in the service of truth, justice, accountability, and democracy itself. Me, retire? No thanks. I'm going to work until I die, even if it kills me, but not at my desk. I want the obituary to begin: "Steve Lopez died on the beat yesterday, chasing a good story on a tight deadline. Cause of death was exhilaration at the thought of tapping out the column, having a cold beer, and then running out on the next one in a crusade that has no end."

There, I did it. A pretty good pro-con list on retirement. But this is why I never mess with lists like this. All that work, and I'm even more confused now.

At least I'm not alone. I'm one of seventy-five million boomers, many of whom are trying to figure out what to do as the clock winds down, and the simple truth is that, for a lot of us, there are no easy or correct answers. You'd think a lifetime of decision-making would sharpen your skills. After all, you muddle through the years deciding what to wear, what to eat, what to drive, what to do for a living, where to live, when to get married, when to get divorced, whether to have kids, and when to kick them out of the house. But none of this helps when it's time to make the toughest remaining decision in your rapidly dwindling life: when to get out of the race.

On days when I'm convinced it's time to go, a smile of freedom crosses my face. Then a big story breaks—the virus, the economic collapse, the marches that echo the sixties—and I'm like a racehorse in the gate, ready to run. In my job, the combination of passion and panic has kept me alive. There's always a task at hand, and I've got to deliver, because the world still needs me.

Doesn't it?

The financial part is a tough enough puzzle on its own, unless you're rich, because you have no idea whether you need your money to last a few years or a few decades. But the part that scares me more than any of that is an even greater unknown.

When I finally walk away, how much of me stays behind?

To paraphrase Robert Louis Stevenson, to be idle requires a strong sense of personal identity.[2] Right now, as a workingman, a husband, and a father, my identity is as clear as my face in the mirror. It's there that I see the spark of inspiration for the next thing I write.

The monster is hungry and has to be fed.

I see inspiration and I see dread.

I can't even remember the last thing I wrote, which might be a sign of creeping dementia, or maybe it's because the job is always about the next one, the next one, and the next one, with no time to look back. The calendar may say I'm old, but the clock says I'm about to be born again. I've got to pay attention, which keeps me invested in the world, in the neighborhood, in the small victories and broken dreams of readers who send me their thoughts, their hopes, their fears, their gripes, their stories. I am alive through them, a member of a community. Some of them send me nice notes and good ideas, and some of them are dead certain I'm an unredeemable idiot, and they are never shy about telling me so.

That's how the mail goes.

The feathers tickle, the darts sting, the blood pumps.

I'm alive.

I once wrote about a Los Angeles algebra teacher who hit forced retirement age, signed all the papers, formally checked out, and then returned to the same school on the first day of the next semester as a volunteer teacher. This teacher knew who he was. Teaching was not a job. It was not a paycheck. It was his identity.

What is mine?

I'm on a mission to figure that out, and I'm inviting you along for the ride. One year. That's my deadline. I'm a reporter, so I'll do what I do. I'll knock on doors and talk to so-called experts. I'll visit people who retired and wish they'd done it sooner. I'll visit people who retired and wish they could claw their way back to where they used to be—to *who* they used to be.

Before it's over, I may also see a shrink, a priest, a rabbi, and a few good bartenders. Maybe a fortune-teller is all I really need.

Enough for now, though. It's a national holiday, and I'm taking the rest of the day off. I'll barbecue burgers in the backyard, bombs bursting in air, and mix some spritz cocktails like the ones we got hooked on in Italy last year. Somewhere out there, on the other side of the smoke, my independence awaits.

TWO

J ULY IS BURNING TO A CLOSE, AND WE'RE ON OUR WAY TO Laguna Beach, a lovely little seaside village an hour away from home. This isn't quite the escape we've been dreaming about, but we had to cancel a trip to Laguna last fall when Caroline got sick, and now we need to use or lose the hotel credit. So here we go, a bit trepidatious about traveling when the virus is so far from being under control, but at least we're not dealing with airports and planes.

In retirement, I plan to do more exploring in California. I was born and raised in the San Francisco Bay Area and have lived in the state for fifty years, but from mountain to sea and from Oregon to Mexico, there's a lot I haven't seen. I recall only one trip to Death Valley, and even then we missed the spring wildflower season that draws people from all over the world. I've visited Yosemite a few times, but never long enough to really, really be there, under its spell and out of my head. I want to explore the Lost Coast above Mendocino, take a slow trek from Mount Shasta to Klamath Basin National Wildlife Refuge, drop down into Lava Beds National Monument. The state is huge, my list is long, my time is short.

We check into a little cottage just north of downtown Laguna late on a Saturday afternoon, and I've got that first-day-of-vacation feeling. In Pasadena, where we live, summer days are sweltering, with temperatures routinely in the nineties and flirting with one hundred, but Laguna is a twenty-degree cooldown. The sun is a stranger in the morning, then pokes through the mist around noon, kissing the brisk blue-green water and rocky outcroppings. Late in the day, the dying sun paints the clouds, and then the marine layer creeps back in for the night. The sound of gulls and the smell of salt air take me back to my childhood vacations in Santa Cruz. In retirement, I intend to spend many days near the water in shorts and flip-flops, and we might even move to a beach town if we can swing it.

On Sunday morning we wake up refreshed, put on sweatshirts, and decide to play tennis before taking a dip in the ocean. This is the life, I tell myself. Carefree, no agenda, no deadlines. But warming up on the high school courts, a bit of reality sets in. My right shoulder and arm ache, as they often do. I don't tell anyone about this, because I don't want to sound like an old man, and I don't tell Alison and Caroline that I forgot to bring my knee braces on the trip. Those joints begin to ache, too, and I'm not playing terribly well, so thank God I don't have to look at myself. A one-minute video of me windmilling about the court is all it would take for me to list all my tennis gear for sale on eBay. My deformed left foot has no arch. It looks more like a ham than a foot, so that's not good. I don't really have much of a game, to be honest, except for a halfway decent serve. So what do I do out here on the court? I serve harder to make up for my shortcomings, and that makes my arm hurt more. It feels as if the tendons and nerves are tangled, bones calcified. Rotator cuff surgery is one option, my doctors have told me. But after what happened to me in knee surgery, when a simple procedure turned into a code blue, no way, and I'll save that story for later.

Playing Alison is like playing a golden retriever. I push her a ball that I feel so good about, I'm ready to count the point, but she gets to it. She almost always gets to it, and yet this comes as a surprise to me every time, leaving me unprepared to handle her return. It's like falling asleep at a bus stop and waking up just as the bus roars away, time after time. With Caroline, that's another story, and the ending is no happier. She effortlessly blasts balls past me. They fly by like bottle rockets on the Fourth of July. But I don't learn from that, either. I keep thinking I'm in the point, in the game, despite unimpeachable evidence to the contrary. I reach, I flail, I tweak my back. Another ball sails past me in a blur, leaving a vapor trail. At least I think that was a ball. I have a blind spot in the lower left center of one eye because of laser surgery to cauterize a bleeding blood vessel. I think to myself, "Why bother retiring? With a rubber arm, a club foot, and a blind spot, it's not like I'm going to get better at tennis with more court time. And if I'm going to be in pain all the time as a retiree, why not forget it and keep getting paid?" Ibuprofen, three at a time, isn't cheap, although if the neuropathy in my foot spreads to the rest of my body, at least I'll save on painkillers.

"It's all about managing decline," my friend Jim Ricci told me, quoting another friend a few years older. It was funny for a moment when Jim said it, but it's been scary ever since. A rather unpleasant way to think about the golden years that lie ahead.

I begin to feel a little better about myself because a couple is playing on the court next to us, and the guy is no better a specimen than I. But that doesn't stop him from trying to coach his wife. You know the type. Do this and don't do that, he says, but nobody in their right mind would pay a nickel for this guy's advice. After a while, another couple shows up, and it turns out they've planned a doubles match. Good for them, but they greet each other like there's no killer virus on the loose. So now I'm thinking, okay, this could be a column. Laguna Beach is in Orange County, one of the epicenters of coronavirus denial. You've got those who say it's a hoax designed to crash the economy and bring down the president. You've got those who say masks don't work or that herd immunity is the best strategy. You've got those who say they have a constitutional right to do as they please. I'm going to get infected by one of these knuckleheads and die before I ever get the satisfaction of cashing a Social Security check.

The column is coming together in my head, but there's one problem—I'm on vacation. Stop working, I tell myself. We've got four nights booked in Laguna, then a few more off days at home, and I really need this break. But when we walk around town or go to the beach or go for a hike in the hills above the stunning expanse of Crystal Cove, we notice that half the people are not distancing or wearing masks. Back at the cottage I check my email, which is what a junkie does on vacation, and a reader has sent me a link to a story in the *Laguna Beach Independent* about a local emergency room doctor who has been blogging on Facebook every day for four months, prodding people to trust science and doctors, not quacks and political opportunists. This is perfect. A good column has fallen into my lap. I do a quick search and find a home number for the doctor. "I have to write this column," my work voice tells me. "No," my vacation voice insists. "You're not on assignment; you're on vacation."

We drive home on Wednesday and I can't help myself. I could do some gardening. I could finish reading a book I've started. I could go on a hike—anything but play tennis, because my right arm feels as if it might have to be amputated after a second day of foolishly hitting through the pain in Laguna. But all I really want to do is call the ER doctor for an interview and tap out a column. I tell myself that if I can't get hold of him, I'll forget it. I leave him two messages with no response. Then he calls back, happy to talk, and I can't wait to start writing. In fact, I spend Thursday morning on my vacation interviewing the mayor of Laguna Beach and doing a little more research, and I spend Thursday afternoon writing the column. I haven't made a decision to do this. It's more like an involuntary response. I tweak the column on Friday morning after thinking, while lying in bed on Thursday evening, about all the ways I could sharpen it. The column gets posted Saturday morning, and seeing it on the website gives me a lift, the same lift I've felt for forty-five years, every time I experience the miracle of seeing my hastily assembled, unformed thoughts get published. It's the greatest scam going.

If this gives me such pleasure, can you even use the word *work* to describe what I do for a living? If I couldn't think of anything I'd rather do while on vacation than call up a doctor and a mayor and write something I thought was important and relevant, maybe I'm already living the perfect life. Is there any good reason to walk away from perfect? I've got a press credential that dangles from my neck. It's a license. It's a passport. It's a chance to meet people, go places, explore, educate myself. I've been to Iraq and Bosnia for stories, to the White House and to prisons, to natural disasters, to forty-eight states and counting, to national political conventions, the Olympics, the Super Bowl. I work in a city where people buy $30 million houses and bulldoze them to rebuild because they don't like the flow, and just down the street, people are living in cardboard boxes.

The news never slows; the show does not close.

Am I a fool to be counting the days to retirement?

I need some help here. Some guidance. I need to hook up with Jim Ricci, the guy who described aging as an exercise in managing decline. Jim, who retired twelve years ago, was a columnist for much of his career, a true wordsmith with a curious mind, a wide range of interests, and a knack for perfectly framing a story. One reason I've been thinking about retiring is that the demands of my job make it hard for me to nurture friendships, like the one I have with Jim, and I've been envious when he's told me about the trips he was taking with mutual friends who are retired, either to catch a ball game or tour another country. I had reached out to Jim recently and asked him what it was like to wake up the day after he retired. Was it liberating? Was it frightening? He said he wanted to think about that for a bit, and then he emailed me this response, which just arrived:

I can't say I have a specific memory of the first day of my retirement, perhaps because I might have cleared out my desk at the *Times* on a Friday, so the next day, Saturday, would have been an ordinary day off, and therefore of no particular resonance.

What I do remember, and this was probably some months later, is a weekday morning during rush hour, driving swiftly in the opposite direction of bumper-to-bumper traffic, and thinking wonderingly, "All those people are going to their jobs... and I'm on my way to play tennis." It took that long for the thought to sink in that I never again had to join that glum cavalcade. Wow. What a feeling.

I had no retirement plans. I thought that having two children, ages nine and seven, at home would provide me with plenty enough opportunity for productive labor on the domestic front, as my wife had a demanding job that required frequent travel.

Besides, I wanted to cook more and drink a lot of wine and read deeply into anything that happened to catch my interest.

I wrote for a living for thirty-seven years. I occasionally nursed thoughts of a big writing project now that I was free of the pestering demands of newspapering. And yet, whenever I actually broached such a project, I found myself stubbornly resisting. Wouldn't it be too much like my former work? Why open myself to all the doubt and self-denigration that was sure to accompany such a venture?

Not writing made me (and still makes me) feel guilty. Oh, I pecked unconvincingly at a film script or two. At one point, I managed to unleash, laboriously, a one-act stage play on the world (well, on a very small corner of it). The process taught me that it would take years of playwriting or screenwriting to achieve even a trace of competence. Did I really care enough to do that?

Tied into the guilt, I think, was a loss of identity in the eyes of others. It had been gratifying to be able to inform a stranger that I was a staff writer for a respected newspaper. It made them look at me with greater respect and curiosity, without my actually having to do anything (and no matter what I actually thought of myself). Being a playwriting dilettante or someone who knew his way around a Bolognese sauce just didn't exalt a person to the same extent.

Nonetheless, I suppose I wanted my retirement to just luff out casually without my having to set benchmarks of achievement to mark its passage. Maybe it would last longer that way, or, at least seem to. Twelve years and counting…

I read Jim's response several times. There's so much in it I can identify with. His guilt about not writing really resonated. In Laguna, I felt guilty about having a column right there in front of me and thinking I should forget about it and just enjoy my downtime. The line of Jim's that really grabbed me, though, was this one: "Tied into the guilt, I think, was a loss of identity in the eyes of others."

Is that what's in store for me?

The urge to write a column on vacation may simply have been a function of not having stepped away long enough to get out of work-think. But what if it was something more than that? What if that urge was akin to chemical dependency? What if it was in my DNA?

My editor, Sue Horton, edited the Laguna Beach column late Friday afternoon. She said it was in pretty good shape and she hadn't done much to it except for a tweak here and there.

"You know," she said, "you're allowed to take a week off without writing."

"I know," I told her. "But how do you do that?"

First thing I did on Saturday morning was check to see how the Laguna Beach column was doing. It was near the top of the home page on our website, which meant it had connected. But on Sunday morning I checked again and it had lost its traction, dropping nearly out of sight.

All I could think about was trying to ace the next one.

THREE

I'M SIFTING THROUGH THE MAIL ONE DAY AND SEE THAT I'VE received another update from the Social Security Administration.

If you're over sixty, you know what I'm talking about. The federal government becomes your pen pal, sending you an annual six-page summary of your anticipated benefits at the time of your retirement. Uncle Sam seems to enjoy reminding you that you're way past your prime, and with each passing year, the pressure mounts to consider the first big decision you have to make as an advancing elder: when to begin drawing Social Security. Once again, as with the question of when to retire, there is no easy answer.

I ignored these mailings when they first began arriving, insulted that the government would think I was on the home stretch. AARP is even more malicious. It starts recruiting you at age fifty—sign up today and get a free sporty tote bag. Your first instinct is to write those bastards a letter telling them what they can do with their tote bag. By about fifty-five, though, the membership discounts at restaurants and movie theaters become more attractive, and the tote bag suddenly seems like it

might make a handsome accessory. You can see yourself dropping a bottle of wine into the tote, along with some cheese and
a box of crackers—and maybe your dentures or blood pressure
medication—and heading to an outdoor concert, at which se-
niors might get 10 percent off on the price of tickets. Yeah, now
we're living, reaping the rewards of our labor.

I know by now pretty much where I stand in terms of monthly
Social Security benefits even before the annual updates arrive.
In my head, the rough numbers are factored into the equation
of my retirement income, which includes two small pensions
from different employers and whatever dividends I might
make on investments. But one of my pension funds is on life
support and may go under. And of course there's no guarantee of any interest on investments. And nobody can calculate
the possibility of unanticipated costs for medical emergencies
or assisted living. And so the Social Security check is the most
solid pillar of my retirement income, although even that is subject to change if Congress decides to trim benefits so the fund
doesn't go under. So each year I tear open the statements a little more eagerly than I did the year before. Maybe a part of me
thinks the federal math wizards are going to say they made a
mistake last time, and my monthly income in retirement will
actually be two or three times what they previously claimed.
But that never happens.

As the statement puts it: "Social Security benefits are not intended to be your only source of income when you retire. On
average, Social Security will replace about 40 percent of your
annual pre-retirement earnings. You will need other savings,
investments, pensions or retirement accounts to live comfortably when you retire."[1]

Okay, thank you very much. I'm actually pretty lucky, based
on statistics, because millions of Americans have little or no

savings even as they approach retirement age, which is one reason some people never get to retire at all.

Page 2 tells you how much your spouse or children will receive monthly "if you die this year." And then, if you pay really close attention to the small print, you'll see this little nugget about a death benefit: "Your spouse or minor child may be eligible for a special one-time benefit of $255."

I don't quite understand the "special" part of this. Is it a limited-time offer, so you better hurry up and kick the bucket? Does the government think that amount of money is special? Do my spouse and child have to split this windfall, or do they each get their own?

"Dear Mrs. Shore: We understand Steve fell off the roof and died while trying to clean the rain gutters. Please accept our condolences, along with this special one-time benefit of $255. Split it with your daughter if you like."

Page 4 lists "Your Earnings Record," and it shocks me every time I look at it, because it says my earnings were first taxed in 1968. I was a teenager then, working for my hometown recreation center as a playground supervisor. And I think to myself, "I've been pounding rocks since the Johnson administration? Why am I not already 'Sitting on the Dock of the Bay'?"[2] (This song by Otis Redding was at the top of the *Billboard* charts in 1968.)

Page 5 asks: "Thinking of retiring?"

Yes, actually. Can you help me out with that?

"Everyone's situation is different," says the pamphlet.

That's what it says. I'm not exaggerating. Your tax dollars made it possible for someone at the Social Security Administration to write that and send it to you in the mail. Everyone's situation is different? Why not just write "red delicious apples usually harvest in September?" It occurred to me that maybe

I could quit my full-time job and write a freelance column for the SSA. They could use my help with some practical, useful information on those mailers. Information such as:

- If you're still answering the home phone, it's time to retire.
- If access to your company email is frozen and you're relatively sure you'll suffer an aneurysm if forced to figure out how to toggle between your phone's Settings icon and your password authenticator app, it's time to retire.
- If you're a male and wake up three times a night to pee, your prostate is the size of a rugby ball, and that's the least of your health problems, so quit your job today and begin drawing Social Security tomorrow.

By the way, a lot of the pamphlet's text is in really small print, like they're messing with you because you're old. The sentences look like trails of ants. I always expect to turn the page and see an ad for Uncle Sam magnifying glasses, with half off the second one if you order now. I'm squinting through drugstore cheaters, so it's a struggle, but I think the next sentence actually says: "If you retire early, you may not have enough income to enjoy the years ahead of you. Likewise, if you retire late, you'll have a larger income, but fewer years to enjoy it."

I think this is a form of elder abuse. They're assuming we're stupid or that our feeble minds have reverted, so we have to be spoken to like kindergarteners. Yeah, we understand the math. The problem is that we have no way to know the most important number of all—how many more years we're going to live. And the reminder from the Social Security Administration isn't really all that helpful.

If you can resist the temptation to begin drawing immediately, says the pamphlet, your ultimate Social Security check will grow by 8 percent a year until you max out at age seventy. That's my plan, but my buddy Greg—who is a year older than I am and still working—advised me to take it early, as he did. The government wants to send you money each month, for free, Greg reasoned, and you're going to say no thanks? If you wait until seventy, he argued, you give up so much money at the front end, you've got to live into your early eighties to make up what you lost. But there is no winning this game, statistically speaking, because the government has done the actuarial work and they know the averages. We're likely to be dead just about the time we draw even.

And there's the rub. What if I wait until seventy to collect the maximum monthly Social Security check, and on the last day of my sixty-ninth year I get hit by a bus? My family will still get a nice check in the mail every month, but I won't be around to see them enjoy my money. That doesn't seem fair. And what if by the end of my sixty-ninth year, I'm not speaking to anybody in my family? What's to keep them from pushing me in front of that bus? I know there have been times when they thought about it, and I've seen *Double Indemnity*, so I keep one eye open when I sleep.

The pamphlet offers the following information to a fence-sitter like me: "You may need your income to be sufficient for a long time, because people are living longer than ever before, and generally, women tend to live longer than men. For example: The typical 65-year-old today will live to age 83. One in four 65-year-olds will live to age 90. And one in ten 65-year-olds will live to age 95."

None of this is helpful in the least, precisely because of the unknowns. I am reminded, though, of my former neighbor Mae, who in her nineties drove an Oldsmobile the size of a yacht, barreled around town reading tea leaves for friends, and became an actress when an agent read one of my columns about her and began representing Mae in movies and commercials. If you've seen *Pineapple Express* or *The Heartbreak Kid* or *It's Always Sunny in Philadelphia*, you probably spotted her, looking something like the woman in the old Wendy's "Where's the beef?" commercials. When Mae hit one hundred, she asked her nephew, an accountant, to take a look at her books because she was afraid she'd soon be down to nothing but her meager Social Security check. Her nephew told Mae not to worry, because she had enough money in the bank to last her until she was 110.

Mae was crestfallen.

"Well, honey," she asked her nephew, "what'll I do then?"

FOUR

M Y SONS JEFF AND ANDREW WERE BORN WHEN I WAS in my twenties, so I could have been an empty nester beginning in my late forties. Their mother and I divorced when they were young and we shared joint custody. But they weren't out of the house long before, in my second marriage, Alison and I began trying to have a baby. I didn't initiate the idea, to be honest. I love being a dad, but with Jeff and Andrew on their own as young adults, I had thought this would be a time for me to change routines rather than change diapers. I suppose you could call me selfish. Alison certainly thought I was, and she held fast.

And then one morning she said she had something to tell me. It wasn't just any morning, either. It was the day I was headed to the medical clinic at UCLA for a colonoscopy, a rite of passage when you turn fifty. I asked Alison if we could talk later, because I had plenty on my mind already. No, she said. This was important.

"Okay, what?"

"I'm pregnant."

Life is rich, but it's not every day that gets punctuated by two such memorable events. A stranger was about to run a periscope through my sewer trap, and I was going to be a father again. At UCLA, I put on the gown, back side open, defenseless against the mounting assault on my liberties. I rolled onto my side and drew my legs up. Here we go. "Give it to me, Doc."

The colonoscopy was negative. The birth was positive. For all my hesitancy about starting over, when Caroline was born, I fell over like a tree in a storm. I wanted to hug her, love her, and drive her home in an armored vehicle to protect her fragile little life. I vowed never to speed again—not one mile an hour above the speed limit—and to drive defensively every moment she was in the car. If she had the sniffles, I wanted to sleep on the floor next to her crib. She was supposed to be a boy, by the way. We didn't want to know the gender before birth, but everyone told us Alison was going to have a son. Look at the way she carried. Look at the fact that she had two brothers and no sisters and the fact that I had two sons and the fact that early in her pregnancy, during a sonogram, the doctor said, "Oh look, you can already see…" We stopped the doctor cold and reminded him we didn't want to know. He apologized and stopped short of revealing any more, but we were all the more certain what he had spotted on the sonogram was the frank and beans. We named our son Benjamin and, for a middle name, we gave him our fathers' first names. He was going to be Benjamin Edward Antonio Lopez. And then, when Benjamin popped out after a long, long, difficult labor, I realized there was no frank and there were no beans.

"Benjamin is a girl," I said, and it was all the more special, because I'd already raised two sons, so this was going to be an entirely new adventure.

One day I went for a walk in the neighborhood with baby Caroline strapped into a harness, her body pressed firmly against me. I felt her chest swell when she saw a flower and then a bird. People had told me having a baby would make me young, and I had responded with a curmudgeonly scoff. But they were right. To hold someone next to me who was excited about the wonder of a flower and a bird was exhilarating. I was as proud as I could be and surprised at how much I looked forward to those days when Caroline was young and innocent and eager to get to school early enough to play soccer or basketball on the playground or to hang out with friends on the climbing equipment. It used to bug me a little bit that I was old enough to be the father of some of the younger dads, and some of those self-satisfied young bucks kept to themselves. But then I figured, so what? On occasion, people would ask me how old my granddaughter was, and that took a little getting used to. But those were some of the happiest days of my life, and I'll never forget that daily ritual of walking to school with the woman I love and our curious, wavy-haired, happy little daughter.

And now here I am, contemplating the fast-approaching empty-nest phase of life, telling myself I'm not ready for this. Where did the time go?

For Alison and me, so much of our day, our week, our lives, is about parenting, about sharing hopes and dreams for our daughter. Vacations have been largely built around her schedule, by necessity. For years, her love of tennis filled our weekends with trips to tournaments. Because of Caroline, Alison and I both took up the sport, and we play each other a couple of times a week. We used to play with Caroline, but she got too good for us and too bored by our inability to keep up with her on a court. And soon she'll be playing tennis in college somewhere. She'll be gone from our daily lives, possibly never to return, except for visits. And in what seems like a flash, I went from hesitancy about having another child to not wanting her to leave. I don't mean that literally, of course. She has to leave, we have to let go, and we will. But what then? The house will be so much quieter, so empty, and a terrifying thought occurs: if I retire when she leaves for college, I'll have two voids to fill, namely, Caroline's departure from home and my departure from work. How am I going to adapt to that?

She's in the college-application process now, and the separation has begun full force. Caroline is private and independent. She wants to figure things out on her own, without much input from us. College coaches text, email, and call her. "We have a spot for you on our roster," says the women's tennis coach at Bard College in New York, and several other schools have reached out. I'm so proud of her and excited for her and worried about the hole in my heart, the hole I'm sure to feel when she's no longer with us at the dinner table, no longer wandering into the living room to tell us something about school or tennis or glee club or the newspaper she and her friends started or her art class or a get-together with her friends. I'll even miss her asking if she can buy stuff—a surfboard, a GoPro, a car. She never runs out of ideas.

At the moment, I'm thinking I'd be a fool to even consider retiring when she leaves. Maybe that'll be the time when I should think about applying for a foreign post at the newspaper or changing my beat to focus exclusively on subjects that hold ever-growing interest for me, such as climate change, social justice, the perils of growing old and having to make difficult decisions, such as when to retire. Maybe, rather than clock out, I could call my column "Golden State," a double entendre, and write about this subject that now occupies so many of my thoughts—growing old, confronting fears, surviving in a world built for the young.

One day Alison and I drive our mutt, Dominic, to the dog beach in Long Beach, and we talk about our future lives as empty-nest parents and what the shape of things will be if I retire right away. Alison, as noted, is never one to hide her feelings. There's no sidestepping, no code words, no detours. On our first date, in Philadelphia, we were on our way to Atlantic City when she told me she read my columns in the *Philadelphia Inquirer* and she thought I was a hypocrite at times, preaching one thing while doing another. I couldn't believe it. First date and she was busting my chops, as they say in Philadelphia, sometimes using another word for chops. I liked it. I liked her spunk. My buddy Robin Clark said at the time that I had found the right mate. "She's got it, pal," he said in his North Carolina drawl. "Looks, smarts, spirit. You hit the trifecta." So on the way to Long Beach the trifecta queen tells me she likes her space, she's always liked her space and her independence and her time and activities with friends, and she's not eager to surrender any of that and spend her days bumping into me in the house as I try to figure out who I am in retirement. She switched from office worker to freelancer as a young adult because she had no patience for office politics and protocol. She wanted to be her own boss, on her own time, in her own place, and that's what she'd been doing ever since, for roughly three decades. So, yes, she said, if I was going to retire, we'd have to work something out. She did not want to give up her alone time.

Okay, I can respect that. But what does it mean? It means that if I retire, I'm going to have to build something I don't have much of now—a social life. I'll need to do more things on my own than I do now, limited as I am by the short leash of my job. Maybe I'll rent a little office somewhere and work on books or freelance stories. I've been asked before to serve on the boards of nonprofits that do all manner of community services. Maybe I should say yes the next time an offer comes my way. There are more ways to be engaged, to be a part of the conversation, to live a life of relevance, than to bang out a couple of columns a week, right? Or maybe I'll just hold onto my job for another year or two. Maybe I've got it all wrong, this idea that I need to figure things out, map my future, know who I am. Does anyone ever really get there? Good grief. Sometimes I feel so confused.

When we get to the beach and walk down to the water's edge, Dominic gets juiced. Ordinarily, on walks through our neighborhood, he's on a leash, and that makes him protective of us and aggressive toward other dogs. At Rosie's Beach, leashes are not required, and the dogs love it. Dominic's mouth is open in what looks like a smile. He races up and down the beach along the water's edge, sniffs the privates of all the other dogs, big and small, and he pees on a woman who's sitting down on the sand with her dog. Dominic has it all figured out. Oh, to be so sure of who you are. To be free.

FIVE

WHEN I HEAR THAT HOMEBOY INDUSTRIES IN LOS Angeles has just won a $2.5 million humanitarian award from the Hilton Foundation, I figure that would make for a sweet column. I also think this would be a good time to catch up with Father Greg Boyle, Homeboy's founder, who happens to be roughly my age and who once told me he didn't plan to retire. Ever.

"Come to my tent," Father Boyle says in an email. "One of the homies told me it feels like the Middle East in here."

Homeboy headquarters is a yellow two-story modern building next to the Gold Line train tracks and across Spring Street from Chinatown. Looking to the northwest, Dodger Stadium is a long home run away, and the skyscrapers of downtown Los Angeles puncture the western sky. Father Boyle's fish-bowl office, just inside the front door, gives him a view of all the comings and goings. But when the coronavirus hit, the homies built an open-air office in the parking lot. They didn't want Father Boyle, whose leukemia has been under a doctor's care for years, to come inside and risk infection.

The billowing white tent is quite grand, a desert oasis with bundled curtains, electric fans, and a woven rug. Father Boyle, his sidewall hair as white as the sleeves of his shirt, sits under the canopy behind an office desk. He's in conversation with staffers seated comfortably before him. Homeboy is the largest gang member rehabilitation and redirection program in the world. Homeboys, or homies, have a choice to make when they leave prison. Go back to the life that landed them in lockup, try to steer clear of trouble on their own, or knock on Father Boyle's door and commit to a new path, get clean, learn a trade, and land a job. It's a two-year program that includes everything from mental health treatment to tattoo removal. You can wager a guess as to how long someone has been a trainee by whether they've undergone the painful experience of having gang affiliations removed from their faces, necks, and shaved heads. Thousands of lives have been saved since the work began in 1986, and the homies are extremely grateful and devoutly protective of L.A.'s patron saint of second chances.

Father Boyle motions me into the tent when his staffers depart, and we begin talking about the humanitarian award—he says it brought him to tears—and generally catching up. He's several months younger than I, and I had told him two years prior that I was beginning to think of moving on. I distinctly remember his response, which was a sort of a visual "Hmm," as if the concept seemed alien to him. He told me he had no interest whatsoever in giving up what was both a mission and a passion, and I held him in even higher regard after hearing that. There's such purity and clarity in his devotion to the young men he serves, young men most of society had given up on or held in contempt.

"Our common human hospitality longs to find room for those who are left out," the padre poet wrote in his first book, *Tattoos on the Heart: The Power of Boundless Compassion.* "Perhaps, to-gether, we can teach each other how to bear the beams of love, persons becoming persons, right before our eyes. Returned to ourselves."[1]

Every once in a while, through the years, Father Boyle has been accused of coddling criminals, but that never breaks his stride. These ex cons, mostly brown and black, may have made terrible decisions and committed horrible crimes, but to this humble man of the cloth, a Jesuit to the core, they are an ex-pression of the violence, poverty, systemic racism, and institu-tional failures that suffocated their neighborhoods and crushed their hopes. He stands with them, tough, demanding, loyal, and many of the homies have never known anyone else who be-lieved they were capable of something good.

"Junior, come here," Father Boyle calls out to a young guy as we're talking. This is a familiar pattern to me. He misses no opportunity to connect with his people, even if he has to apologize for interrupting an interview. "Here's the thing, son. I want you to show up Wednesday morning right here. I want to be here when you start."

"Okay, I'll be here at seven," the trainee replies.

"No," Boyle says. "That's too early."

This guy has been through the program before and fell away. Now he's giving it a second try, Father Boyle tells me, and he wants to be there from day one to let him know he's rooting for him and expecting a better result this time.

A man in his thirties named Joseph spots Father Boyle and marches over to the tent. He apologizes for the interruption but says he couldn't wait to tell the padre what had just hap-pened. He'd been through Homeboy's solar panel training pro-gram and he'd just landed a job. In the early days of Homeboy, one of the slogans was "Nothing stops a bullet like a job."

"It's thirty-four dollars an hour," says Joseph, chest puffed with pride. Father Boyle had baptized him when he was ten years old and locked up in a detention camp, Joseph tells me. He didn't trust himself to be able to turn his life around, but he kept the faith, along with the connection to Father Boyle.

Boyle congratulates him, taps his own heart, and says, "Love you, son."

Another trainee, a guy I'd met at Homeboy a couple of years ago, spots us and comes by to say hello. He'd been a member of one of L.A.'s most notorious gangs, MS-13, and he said the lure of money from drug sales had been a powerful force in his life. But he's here now, looking for something more soul-sustaining than easy money. He'd just had a baby, Father Boyle is going to perform the baptism, and they have a few details to work out.

"Don't you love this, Pops?" the young man asks his mentor, gesturing to the majesty of the tent.

"It's nice," says Boyle. "But I miss the action inside."

I'm no Father Boyle. I don't have his fortitude, but if I were to summarize the point of what I do, it's to stand up for social and economic justice, to stand with and speak up for those whose stories need telling. I'd like to think that, on some level, Father Boyle and I understand each other in that regard. I remind him of our brief chat on retirement two years earlier and tell him I'm still thinking about it, but I'm torn. I'd be gaining something if I retire, but can I afford to lose what I already have?

"The baseline," Father Boyle says, "is to go where life is, and as long as this gives you meaning, why would you stop?"

The newspaper business has taken a beating, I tell him. And on some days, the job isn't as rewarding as it once was. I'd like to know what it feels like to do something else.

"Sometimes you're diminished," he says, and maybe he's expressing how his own job has tested him at times. He keeps a running count of the young people he has buried—it's in the hundreds. But Father Boyle quickly pivots back to the strength his job gives him. "You wanna stay anchored in loving and tethered to a sustaining God and, you know, be mindful of the goodness in people," he tells me. "For me that's eternally replenishing, and you have to do what replenishes you."

So would he ever retire?

Father Boyle doesn't need to think it over.

"Jesuits retire in the graveyard," he says.

—⁓—

Go where life is and find meaning. Do what replenishes you. Wise words, but retiring wouldn't necessarily deprive me of the chance to be fulfilled in other ways. I tucked Father Boyle's advice away and went about my next story, which involved a bit of a departure from my regular work routine. For decades, the *L.A. Times* has had a popular news feature called "Column One," which runs on the front page and takes a look at someone or something in greater depth than what can be accomplished in a regular story or column. My editors told me it would be okay to skip the occasional column and devote that time to longer "Column One" features. This would be a nice change of pace, and I'd had a "Column One" idea kicking around in my head on the topic of climate change ever since a conversation two years earlier with one of California's legendary winemakers.

Alison and I had dropped Caroline off at a weeklong summer tennis camp at UC Santa Cruz—a good opportunity for her to work with college coaches, crash in university dorms, and get some match time with other rising players. Alison and I rented a cabin in the rustic Santa Cruz mountain town of Ben Lomond, and we didn't have much of an agenda. Sleep late.

Relax. Read. Enjoy the clean mountain air and the majesty of towering coastal redwoods. The kinds of things I imagine myself doing all the time in retirement. One day we drove to the coast for a wine tasting with Randall Grahm of Bonny Doon Vineyard. Grahm, bespectacled and ponytailed, is often reverentially referred to by colleagues as a genius winemaker. In a state where the big-money grapes are cabernet sauvignon, chardonnay, and pinot noir, he made his name by going in a different direction, renegade that he is. He planted the grapes of France's southern Rhône Valley—Mourvédre, Grenache, and Syrah, among others—and produced red blends that were big hits critically and commercially, including Big House Red, Cardinal Zin, and Le Cigare Volant ("Flying Cigar"). In 1989, Grahm was on the cover of *Wine Spectator*, which bestowed on him a moniker that would stick: the Rhône Ranger.

At the tasting, Grahm brought out bottle after bottle of wine, splashed an inch or so into his glass and ours, and took a sip. He wasn't interested in swallowing, just in testing whether he was pleased with his creation. So he kept spitting fine wine into a bucket, which struck me as sinful. I swallowed all of mine. I'm no wine expert, so being with Grahm was a little intimidating. About halfway through our visit, Grahm said something that sounded to me like a good story. He said there was far less fog creeping in from Monterey Bay, flushing through the redwoods and cooling his grapes, than there had been twenty-five years earlier. Climate change was not an abstract idea for him but something he could see. Something that was threatening some of the most popular grapes and growing regions in the state, including Napa Valley cabernet sauvignon, the king of California grapes.

That stuck with me, the idea of the grape as another canary in the climate-change coal mine. And I decided to make that the subject of my first "Column One." I spent several days inter-viewing winemakers and climate scientists by phone and read a Stanford University study, from way back in 2011, that pre-dicted a 50 percent shrinkage of prime wine-growing land in Northern California by 2040 because of increasingly extreme heat and sunlight.[2] In numerous ways, it's all pretty frighten-ing. I grew up just east of San Francisco, and on summer out-ings to the city we'd bundle up, knowing that we were traveling from ninety degrees to sixty cold, foggy degrees in just an hour. But this year, in June, the temperature reading at San Francisco International Airport was a record-shattering one hundred de-grees. California's summers have become hot and smoky, with massive wildfires burning out of control, devouring homes, and forcing evacuations. A subtler but significant impact is the threat to California's $40 billion, thirty-thousand-employee wine industry, the fourth largest producer in the world and maker of 80 percent of the wine in the United States.[3] Already, warming and erratic patterns of drought and deluge associated with climate change had struck a conversation among wine-makers about adopting climate-resistant growing techniques and switching to more heat-resistant grape varieties.

When my preliminary reporting was done, it was time to hit the road for some face-to-face interviews. Seven hours of driving lands me in the quaint Napa Valley town of Calistoga, where I grab a quick meal and go to bed, knowing I have an early start the next day. Before dawn, I meet up with a wine-maker who has been sounding the alarm on climate change. I go to a harvest with him, watch a dozen men snip grapes from the vine, and then I watch as the winemaker maneuvers a fork-lift and dumps the grapes into a press.

The closer I get to retirement, the less I take such expe-riences for granted. It's a privilege, really, to be able to call a winemaker and say, "Hey, I'd like to hang out with you in the vineyards, watch a harvest, and talk to you about great wine and how to survive climate change." This beats the hell out of real work, and, in fact, I've never had what could be called a real job. It's been nothing but this for almost half a century: me wandering around, finding what looks interesting, assembling a story, and moving on to the next. After the harvest, I drive to Napa to meet with another winemaker to talk about the threat to pinot noir and how he's using shading techniques and artificial intelligence to fight climate change. My next stop is the Santa Cruz Mountains, where I stand on the edge of the San Andreas fault with a winemaker who gazes out at rows of cabernet and explains that this higher elevation seems safe, for now, from climate change. It's cooler up here and the grapes like that.

I begin the next morning with a walk along the cliffs in Santa Cruz, looking out at literally hundreds of surfers lined up and waiting for the next sets to roll in. Ninety minutes later I'm in San Juan Bautista, whose claim to fame is that the scary scenes from the Hitchcock movie *Vertigo*, with Jimmy Stewart and Kim Novak, were shot here. Just outside of town, in a vineyard set on rising terrain, I meet up with the Rhône Ranger.

Randall Grahm told me he first saw this 280-acre plot of land in a dream, and this is where he is working on a project more ambitious than anything he's ever done. California's best wines don't say enough about where they're from, he explains as he leads me on a tour of his land. They say something about the grape, but not the specifics of the place. He wants to create *a vin de terroir*, he says in a French accent, and to do so, he is breeding grapes of multiple varieties in an attempt to create a new variety that is, among other things, built to withstand climate change.

Sometimes, when I'm reporting, I begin piecing the story together in my head. I know this one will begin with Grahm telling me two years ago that there was less fog on Monterey Bay than there used to be, and I know it will end here, with him in his laboratory, working, sweating, dreaming. It's hard for me to explain how fulfilling it is to see a story take shape, especially when it's a story about something I feel strongly about, such as climate change. As we walk through his vineyard, he misses nothing. He carries clippers on his belt and kneels frequently to snip a growth that might be shading a cluster of grapes that needs more sun. There's love in what he does, as if he is looking after his children. I can see it in his eyes. He picks a grape from a Grenache vine, tastes it, and mutters favorably. He gives me one, and it's sweet and tart on the tongue, perfection in progress.

After the tour, Grahm leads me up a dusty trail to an overlook. He grabs a cooler case out of his car, and we sit at a picnic table overlooking his vineyard, which he calls Popelouchum, or "paradise" in the language of the Native Americans who once lived here. As he had two years earlier at his tasting room next to the sea, an hour from this spot, Grahm brings out bottle after bottle of wine, and we sample them while looking out at paradise. It'll be years before he crosses and marries the stalks to create his new grape, and it's not even a certainty that he can achieve that dream. But Grahm is trying, which is the part I really admire. And the wine from his early plantings is damn good.

Maybe it's the wine and the company, maybe it's the view, maybe it's a recognition of time's uncompromising advance. But I'm thinking about Father Greg and Randall Grahm and how sweet it is that I can drop in on them. In retirement, a visit with Father Boyle would just be me getting in the way of a workingman. Randall Grahm might politely allow me to drop by, but why would a man chasing a dream make time for a slumming pensioner?

Grahm, like Father Boyle, is my age. I tell him I've been thinking about retiring, but as I sit there, drinking wine with him and hearing about his passion, I can't imagine doing anything in retirement that would be more enjoyable. He nods and says he might not be around to see his work completed here at this vineyard. But if it gets off to a good start, he says, someone else might be able to build on his dream.

He tells me his knees ache, and he wonders how many more times he can crouch under a vine to prune it or examine its berries. But he has no plans to give this up.

"I'm going to die in the vineyard," the Rhône Ranger tells me.

SIX

Today, August 23, is my birthday.

But not my first one, which is in October.

Allow me to explain, because what happened to me exactly eight years ago today is never far from my mind, especially when I consider the pros and cons of retiring within the next year.

I was fifty-eight and reasonably healthy, except for a pair of decrepit, arthritic knees. I'd tried every remedy there was—painkillers, physical therapy, and steroid injections—all of which offered only temporary relief. I'd seen an ad in an in-flight magazine for tissue regeneration and asked my doctor about it, but he said forget it. I'd lost so much cartilage, I was bone on bone on the medial side of both knees, with no better option than partial replacements. In my humble opinion, I was too young for joint replacement. But the number of such surgeries was skyrocketing, my doctor said, because more people are older than ever in history, and more people are physically active in middle age and beyond, which is good for the heart but hell on the joints. We decided to fix the left knee first, and after a few months of recovery, do the right.

Before the sun rose on the day of my first surgery, I got up and called for a cab to take me to the hospital. Alison would stay home with Caroline, then come check on me after the surgery and bring me home in a day or two. But my cab didn't show, even after I called again. Maybe I should have taken this as a sign. Instead, I raced to the hospital in my own car, making it just in time to not forfeit my spot on the knee-replacement assembly line. The medical assistants were awfully cheery in surgical prep. This helped take my mind off a sobering reality. The legs that had carried me through the first fifty-eight years of my life were no good anymore, and one of them was about to be sliced open so the surgeon could saw through the bone and bolt an artificial knee into place. The whole thing sounded barbaric, so I tried to think more pleasant thoughts. But then the staff asked if I had brought my advance healthcare directive with me, in case something went wrong. A legal formality, right? People don't die from knee surgery, do they?

The sedation kicked in quickly, the doctor did his handi-work, and a few hours later, I was safely out of surgery and rest-ing comfortably in post-op. Although heavily drugged, I had a perfectly lovely conversation with the nurse who watched over me. Andrew Fabella said he was from a nursing family. His wife was a nurse, too, he said, and we talked about our chil-dren. I told Andrew I had two sons, thirty-four and thirty-two at the time, and a daughter who was nine. My advice, by the way, is that in your family planning, you should keep the spac-ing tighter than I did. Having a quarter of a century between your youngest and eldest offspring means you may never, ever retire with money in your pocket and time on the clock. You may well have to work until the day you die, which, as I was about to discover, can come sooner than you think.

After dreading the thought of this leg-chopping ordeal, I was relieved to have survived surgery. One knee replacement down, one more to go. And then I'd hike trails. I'd climb mountains. I'd shoot baskets with my daughter. Get back out on the tennis courts. At the prospect of a new life, a mellow giddiness came over me, an intoxicating balm of relief, pain-killing opioids, and anesthesia vapor trails. Nurse Fabella asked me how I was doing, and I said I was fine, just a bit whipped. Flat on my back, I gazed in the direction of the heavens, through the gauzy smear of overhead light. I closed my eyes and time disappeared. I was weightless, untethered, floating through the portal and into the abyss.

And gone. Quite literally.

I was dead.

My heart rate had slowed and then stopped. I was a victim of cardiac arrest, and my gurney had become my coffin. I should have canceled the surgery when the cab didn't come. Goodbye loved ones. Goodbye cruel world. Goodbye one and all. Without so much as a chance to order one more for the road, I was finished.

—∿—

When I opened my eyes, I saw ten sets of eyes looking down at me. I was surrounded by doctors and nurses who, moments earlier, had been staring at a cadaver.

"How do you feel?" someone asked.

"Okay," I said. "Why?"

Nurse Fabella told me I had flatlined.

What?

Fabella said I had appeared to be doing fine, so he moved over to another patient who'd just been wheeled into post-op.

Another nurse checked on me and called out to Fabella, asking what my heart rate had been because, all of a sudden, it was dropping fast.

If you suffer cardiac arrest outside a hospital, good luck. The survival rate is about 10 percent. Even if it happens in a hospital, your odds aren't good. About 25 percent pull through. Unlike heart attacks, which involve plumbing issues, cardiac arrest is an electrical malfunction, and it is a huge killer. About 350,000 people in the United States die each year of cardiac arrest.[1]

They did not bring out the defibrillator paddles, the ones that deliver a jolt of electricity so forceful the body flops like a lunker fished out of water. Instead, acting quickly, Fabella had hunched over me to begin chest compressions, thrusting with all his weight. I was not dead for long. The estimates varied later, but it's likely I was gone less than a minute before coming back from the beyond.

After I was stabilized and moved to another unit, teams of doctors began showing up to have a look at me. I remember an anesthesiologist, a cardiologist, my knee surgeon. I remember nurses coming and going and discussions, at the foot of my bed, about what had gone wrong. The fact that they couldn't pinpoint a cause was more than a little disconcerting. Alison was by my side after a while, along with a couple of my colleagues from the *Los Angeles Times*. I remember their telling me to take it easy and not even think about when I might return to work.

Were they nuts?

How many journalists get a chance to write about their own death? I wanted my laptop so I could get to work, but the repaired knee was beginning to throb and my chest ached. Why did my chest hurt so badly, I wondered, after knee surgery? Oh, yeah. The chest compressions. They wheeled in an X-ray machine to see if a rib had been cracked, the first of several such scans. Instead of going home in a day or two, which is the normal procedure after a knee replacement, I'd be stuck in the hospital several more days for observation, I was told. I had written half the column before the operation, anticipating that the piece would be about recovering from successful knee surgery, with tips for other hobbled boomers. But now I had a much better story to work with, and so, propped up in bed with a tube draining fluid out of my grotesquely swollen knee, I took hold of my laptop and wrote about coming back from the dead. My friend Mark, an ER doctor, told me I had a new birthday.

So what really did trigger my flatlining experience in post-op? Prior to surgery, I had to be cleared for takeoff by a cardiologist, because I have a history of high blood pressure and arrhythmia. It runs in my family, and both my parents had significant heart issues at the time of their deaths. My arteries were clear, I'd been told after a stress test prior to surgery. But cardiac arrest can be triggered by trauma or stress or even by anesthesia, and my body had all those things during knee surgery. Cardiac arrest usually occurs when the electrical malfunction causes ventricular tachycardia, a speedup of the heart rate, or ventricular fibrillation. In my case, the malfunction caused an extreme slowing of the heart, or bradycardia. Could it happen again? Yes. Anywhere, anytime. My cardiologist recommended implanting a pacemaker to prevent such an event. If the heart tries to drop below a certain rate, say fifty or sixty beats per minute, the pacemaker jump-starts the heart.

A week after entering the hospital, I went home with twice as much hardware as I had bargained for. I had a new knee, with weeks of physical therapy ahead of me and another knee replacement in a few months. And I had a pacemaker, with a matchbook-size protrusion on my chest, under the left shoulder. I hated the feel of it under my fingers, and I hated the way the device stretched the skin to accommodate the bulge. It was a constant reminder of what had happened and of my mortality. By virtue of what I do for a living, there isn't a lot of time for reflection. The next deadline is always fast approaching, so I keep my head down, do the work, move on to the next assignment. But what happened in the hospital shook me. When I got home, I remember looking at Alison and Caroline and thinking about how lucky I was and how quickly and unexpectedly you can lose everything that matters.

In the fall of 2019, I went to Italy with a Los Angeles delegation studying a mental health treatment program that was going to be the inspiration for a pilot in Hollywood. Next to me on the plane home was a guy roughly my age, and next to him was a woman—presumably his wife—who had to help him fasten his seat belt. He was fair and slight, with a hairless dome and eyes the color of the Adriatic. His medical condition made it difficult for him to speak or move. I don't know what the diagnosis might have been. Maybe Parkinson's or Lou Gehrig's disease. Maybe he had suffered a stroke.

The woman must have taken a sedative, because she soon fell into a deep sleep, leaving the man next to me to fend for himself. A flight attendant brushed by and asked if anyone needed anything, but before the man could turn his head in her direction and attempt to squeeze out a word, she was gone. I asked him if I could help. He turned, ever so slowly, to face me. It was work for him to move or to speak. He whispered something I didn't understand. I pointed to the television in front of him. He nodded. I pulled the remote control out of its side pocket and turned on his TV, and then cradled his headset into place on his head. He strained to meet my eyes, a thank-you gesture, I think. The poor soul must have been wearing diapers, because during the long flight my prostate took me to the loo several times while he just sat, dozing off occasionally and then opening his eyes to stare into the void. I wondered as we crossed oceans and mountains what his life might have been, what had gone wrong, whether he'd live differently if he had another chance. But mostly I was turned inward, selfishly preoccupied with my own mortality. "This could be me," I thought. This could be any of us.

Shortly after my brief death in 2012, my new knee was pretty good but still swollen when we went to Hawaii for Thanksgiving. I had learned the basics of beginner surfing a couple of years earlier, when it dawned on me that it was sinful to grow up in California and never ride a wave. In Hawaii, even with an arthritic right knee and a left knee still stiff and swollen from surgery, I wanted to ride just one wave at Waikiki rather than regret not taking the chance. And so I did, and it was a thrill I'll never forget.

The waves at Waikiki, when they're not too big, are perfect for beginners on the sturdy, soft-top longboards you can rent on the beach. Once you're standing, thrust morphs into balance, and you feel like you know what you're doing on long-rolling, forgiving waves. The Diamond Head crater is off to your right as you glide toward the beach, riding the miracle of an ancient force that makes you young. I felt triumphant, having survived a brush with death and having confronted the fear of being thrown by a wave. It was all the more exhilarating because Alison and Caroline were riding the waves alongside me, smiles all around. I felt blessed, awed, renewed.

A few months later, I had the second knee replaced and suffered none of the potential negative side effects, including death.

What do you do with a second chance?

Do you eat nothing but nuts and berries and live cleanly in hopes of buying a little more time?

Do you order more chips and guac and another pitcher of margaritas because we're all on borrowed time?

Do you cash it all in and become a surf bum?

Or do you give in to the possibility that you're no different from Father Greg, who intends to retire in the graveyard, and Randall Grahm, who intends to die in the vineyard?

On August 23, 2012, back from the dead, I began searching for answers that still elude me.

Eight years later, happy birthday to me.

And many more.

SEVEN

M Y SON JEFF WORKS IN DIGITAL ADVERTISING, AND LIKE a lot of other people, he began working from home in the last year. And he wondered if it really mattered where he lay his head at night as long as he got his work done. Would it be okay, he wondered, if he went to visit his mother in Philadelphia and work from there? Sure, his boss said. Why not?

Jeff, forty-two, headed east just before Thanksgiving. Almost immediately, it was harder than usual for me to get hold of him by phone, text, and email. His work schedule is pretty demanding, so, at first, I attributed the radio silence to that. But when we finally talked by phone, he mentioned he had gone out with a woman he hadn't seen in decades.

Do you get where I'm going with this? Jeff was hard to get hold of because, as he put it, he was falling in love. And it turns out that he's not coming back to Los Angeles except to pack his bags and move to Philadelphia, after living in L.A. for fifteen years.

What goes around comes around, as they say. When I was a young man, my parents were heartbroken when I left

California for the East Coast. They knew they wouldn't see nearly as much of me or their grandsons as they had. But by the time I made the move, in the 1980s, it was far more common for families to splinter like that, partly because it was no longer the norm in a mobile society for people to work for a single employer for an entire career. In my case, I was moving from the *San Jose Mercury News* to the *Philadelphia Inquirer*, and my sons grew up primarily in Philadelphia. Then Jeff ended up going to school in San Francisco, and Andrew in London. At the time, I wanted them to have those experiences, discover new places, grow their independence. But the older I get, the softer I am. I wanna see my boys more than I do now. It's going to be difficult now with both of them on the East Coast (Andrew is in New London, Connecticut). And there's breaking news here at Casa Lopez.

Caroline may soon be moving into the same time zone as her brothers, because two weeks before Christmas, she got an early present. She's been accepted at Bard College in New York.

This is cause for a huge sigh of relief in our house. Caroline applied to ten colleges, and we knew she'd get into one or more of them. But Bard was near the top of her list, and this process is so drawn out and nerve-racking, you just don't know what's going to happen until it happens. Caroline liked the academic offerings at Bard, and the tennis coach had assured her a spot on the 2021 roster.

Caroline texts us her big news from tennis practice, and she'll be home in an hour or two. I quickly rummage around for a felt marker and some poster board. I look up Bard to find out what the school mascot is and, unfortunately, it's a raptor, which I know I'm not going to be able to draw very well. But I give it my best and write "Congratulations Bard Raptor" on the poster, decorate the whole thing with curled red ribbon, and hang my creation from the lamp over the kitchen table. I stand back to admire the work and realize the raptor looks more like a sea lion and not a very healthy one at that. But it's the thought that counts. I call a local bakery with one-hour delivery and order her favorite dessert, tiramisu, and Alison and I wait for the young Raptor to walk in the door.

When Caroline was younger, Alison and I would be a wreck about dropping her off at a camp for a week. We'd urge her to get in touch and let us know how things were going, and then we'd hear nothing at all. She was engaged and having a good time, and the whole point was to get away from routine and try something different. When the college selection process began, she made clear at the outset that she was not a kid who wanted much input from her parents. She wanted us to be available as sounding boards now and again, but she was intent on figuring things out on her own. Alison and I are both writers, but our daughter didn't want us to edit her college essays. She wanted them to be about her, by her, and without language or ideas that looked as if they might have come from an adult. She wanted to get into a college or not on her own terms and abilities. And her only objective, in terms of geographic location, was to be far from home. This isn't an act of rejection or rebellion, we don't think. It's a product of Caroline having done a lot of traveling, inside and outside the United States, and not wanting to limit her search to a single area.

Caroline is beaming when she arrives. For her, too, the pressure is off after a year of anticipating, planning, and sorting. Bard is artsy, it's political, it's in New York, and it has some cachet. It also comes with a $70,000-a-year price tag, but I'm trying not to dwell on that at the moment. None of us have ever visited the school, and that's one of the unfortunate byproducts of the pandemic. Caroline and her classmates could be forced to make one of the most important decisions of their lives without an opportunity to see the colleges on their lists. But we know from multiple accounts that Bard has a beautiful campus, and we know Caroline's academic interests align with a program there. If she gets into no other school, it'll be okay.

Caroline is drenched in sweat after her practice, but so what? Alison and I hug and congratulate her.

Of course, I'm thrilled, proud, and relieved.

And a little bit sad.

Caroline won't leave the house for another nine months, but this exciting piece of news has put us one step closer to the reality of her departure. And I'm thinking that if I retire next year, I will be an empty nester with no day job and none of my three adult children living anywhere nearby. So, if I seriously intend to retire and inherit unlimited free time, I need to get far more serious about answering one very important question: What the hell am I going to do all day?

When people are surveyed about what they want in retirement, some of the top responses include financial survivability, travel, volunteering, new experiences, and time with family. In fact, the Grandparent Study, a 2002 report by AARP, said eight out of ten grandparents want to live near their children and grandchildren.[1] For some retirees, no doubt, that's a good choice. But would it be for me?

Like the idea of retirement itself, I'm conflicted. It would make sense, in some ways, to move back to New York City or Philadelphia, two cities where Alison and I lived pre-Caroline, before moving to Los Angeles twenty years ago. I love New York, although it might be too expensive to live in the city in retirement. But I have plenty of friends on the East Coast, and when I lived in Philadelphia, summers on the Jersey Shore made for some of my greatest experiences and memories. Also, Alison is from Pennsylvania, where her mother and brothers still live, and some of her best friends are on the East Coast. Another big advantage to such a move would be financial. We could sell our California house, which sits in one of the many ridiculously priced areas of greater Los Angeles, and carve out more financial security with a less expensive home somewhere on the East Coast. Not a week goes by without my checking real estate listings in Cape May, New Jersey, a sweet little town that would put us just a couple of hours from Philadelphia and a half-day's drive from Andrew in Connecticut and Caroline at Bard. The most important advantage to such a move would be that Alison would get to see much more of her mother, Nancy, who is in her late eighties. Alison loves her mother dearly and would be delighted to spend more time with her.

But the last thing I want to do, in the case of my two sons and daughter, is to hover. You rear them, you love them even when they make you want to rip out what's left of your hair, and then you have to stand back and let go, even if you find yourself blubbering at the sight of them waving goodbye. Caroline has been stuck with us for going on eighteen years, and as I said, her instinct in applying to college was to fear nothing—not the cold, not the distance, not the absence of a single familiar face. To be honest, if she were to leave for Bard in August, and Alison and I moved to New York a month later, she'd probably be horrified and possibly transfer as soon as possible. And there's one more argument for Alison and me to stay put in California. Just because Caroline might go to college on the East Coast doesn't mean she's going to stay there, so there's no real percentage in our trying to follow her around.

Later on, who knows? Let's say Caroline graduates, begins a career, gets married, has children, and decides she'd like those kids to get to know their grandparents. Okay, I could go for that, but then you're entering an entirely more challenging kind of family dynamic. There's no way to put this diplomatically or gently, so I'll just say it. What if your grown child is a lousy parent and your grandchild is an incorrigible brat? The possibilities for clashes are limitless, so a smart grandparent ought to think twice about living just down the street or even across town from that kind of trouble.

When I was the gray-bearded old-timer at Caroline's elementary school, many of the young hipster parents struck me as self-indulgent, if not clueless. If their kid regularly disrupted class and was called out by the teacher, it wasn't because the child was an ill-bred little snot. It was because the child was brilliant and, of course, unchallenged by a teacher who was too dim-witted to recognize the child's singular talents. They're all little geniuses with food allergies, so they eat nothing but kale chips and wildflowers, for which many of them are named, and you can't say no to them about anything. They could poop on the floor or set fire to the cat, and you can't say, "No, Chrysanthemum, don't do that," because their creative instincts will be stunted if you set boundaries or confine them to a conventional desk and expect them to keep their little traps shut while the teacher is talking. And it doesn't take long to realize the parents don't even necessarily think their spoiled cubs are all that smart; they're just exploiting the little devils. What they're really telling you is that their kids have to be brilliant, because, of course, the parents are brilliant.

So no, I'm not saying Caroline will be a lousy parent and raise an annoying brood. I'm just saying it's worth thinking twice before I move in across the street from her and sign up for on-call duty. With closeness like that, it won't be long before grandpa is tapping the retirement fund to pay for every little thing. The AARP study said 52 percent of grandparents help out with their grandchildren's educational expenses, 45 percent help with living expenses, and 25 percent help with medical or dental expenses.[2] So there's that to look forward to: the possibility that you will be guilted into forgoing dentures or hearing aids because your granddaughter needs orthodontia.

So you want the truth?

The truth is, I'm a softie. I'd love to cuddle a grandkid now and again, and I'd be willing to relocate at some point. But until further notice, I think that no matter where Caroline goes to college, I'm going to stay put here in Pasadena. For now, anyway. If we learned anything during the pandemic, thanks to Zoom and other videoconferencing programs, it's that none of us can ever again escape each other.

EIGHT

PSYCHOLOGIST NANCY SCHLOSSBERG DIDN'T SET OUT TO become a go-to authority, author, and lecturer on the subject of retirement. It happened somewhat accidentally, beginning with her own retirement in her late sixties, which opened the door to a new career she'd never envisioned.

"The most amazing thing is that I'm ninety-one," she told me just before turning ninety-two, "and that is a mind-blowing number. When you think about a ninety-year-old, you think about someone who no longer works or is that active."

Schlossberg is one of those people who make you think, "Please, Lord, if only I could be half as sharp as she is if I live as long as she has." Recent business has been good for Schlossberg, who has almost twenty-five years on me and sounds like she's twice as busy. The hassle of crowded airports and planes has made her frequent trips to consulting jobs far less appealing. But the world still comes knocking at Schlossberg's door, and clients are happy enough to have her conduct seminars remotely. So, from her home office, it is one teleconference after another, with Schlossberg juggling six contracts, including a series of presentations for Massachusetts state judges forced to retire at age seventy.

Schlossberg, by the way, didn't make a particularly smooth transition when she said goodbye to a long career as a counseling psychologist on the faculties of Howard University, Wayne State, and the University of Maryland, where she taught for twenty-six years in the school's College of Education and researched the lives of adults in transition. That might have been because she more or less gave up her job on a whim.

"I went to the retirement party of a wonderful woman professor, and I was walking back to the office with two male deans," Schlossberg said. "They were talking about how this other woman should have retired sooner. And I'm thinking, 'Nobody's going to ever say that about me. And maybe it's time to really think about leaving.'"

She did the leaving part just fine, but not the "really think" part.

"I thought it was going to be a piece of cake, because I was an expert in transitions. I had a husband I loved and I had a lot going for me," Schlossberg told me. "But it turned out to be very difficult."

Schlossberg didn't stop working entirely after quitting the faculty at Maryland. Among other new ventures, she had taken on a project in which she and a few colleagues were studying a trend in which more grandparents were raising their grandchildren, in many cases because the parents of the kids were deemed unfit for one reason or another or were too young to know what they were doing. Schlossberg found that, in many cases, the financial and mental tolls on the grandparents were significant, with the grandchildren suffering just as much as their caretakers. All of this proved to be interesting work for Schlossberg, but it didn't necessarily put to rest her uneasiness about who and what she'd be after a long career with a weekly paycheck, a community of colleagues, and a sense of belonging.

"A reporter called to interview me," Schlossberg told me, "and he wanted to know how to identify me, and I gagged. I absolutely gagged because I didn't know what to say. Up until a month earlier I was a tenured, full professor at the University of Maryland who had written several books, and now someone is asking me who I am, and I had no idea what to say. After I stammered, I said something like, oh, I'm a consultant or something like that."

Schlossberg says she thought about the business card she used to carry in her university job, which clearly identified who and what she was. Suddenly those cards were scrapbook items, and she didn't know what she'd say about herself if she had new cards printed. Schlossberg was in the midst of something she'd never anticipated: an identity crisis. She and her husband, Steve, who had been an executive with the autoworkers union, moved out of their longtime home in Maryland and bought a place in their frequent vacation destination, Sarasota, Florida. Though she was more than a little familiar with the central Gulf Coast area, she had left behind many of the social connections, routines, and other support systems that give life meaning. Schlossberg frequently uses a word to describe what many retirees are looking for, whether they know it or not. They want to matter, she says. Even for those who are content to sit in a chair with a remote control, there's got to be a connection to something. Mattering, Schlossberg said, is a basic human need. Do you matter to loved ones? To a pet? To friends? To former colleagues who look up to you for sage advice? For all her past achievements, Schlossberg found in Florida that she needed to find new ways to matter.

"I thought every nonprofit would be dying to have me work for them, but all I got asked to do was to be on boards. The whole thing was so upsetting, I thought, 'I better learn something about retirement.'"

And so it began. A new chapter, a new purpose, a life of meaning. And of mattering.

Schlossberg began interviewing retirees who lived in trailer parks and senior housing facilities, and she found publishers who were interested in her marrying her study of transitions with her quest to understand retirement as one of the biggest transitions any adult will ever experience. In 2003, she published *Retire Smart, Retire Happy: Finding Your True Path in Life*,[1] a study of the psychological and emotional adjustments people make in retirement. Six years later, she published *Revitalizing Retirement*,[2] and in 2017, she added another guide to retiring boomers. This one was titled *Too Young to Be Old: Love, Learn, Work, and Play as You Age*.[3] She established a consulting agency, called TransitionWorks, wrote about the topic for major publications, and was a featured expert in a PBS series based on *Retire Smart, Retire Happy*.

So much for putting her feet up. Schlossberg just isn't that kind of retiree, if you can call her a retiree at all. Her daughter, a goat farmer, made an astute observation about Schlossberg's reinvention.

"She said, 'The only thing retired about you is your paycheck.'"

Nancy told me that, through years of study, she had identified six general categories of retirees.

- Continuers who fit existing skills to some modified use.
- Easy gliders who proceed without a plan and take each day as it comes.

- Adventurers who make big changes and try completely new things, some of them daring.
- Searchers who reflect on the meaning of the lives they've lived as they contemplate what to do in their remaining years.
- Involved spectators who remain committed to their career field but find different forms of engagement.
- Retreaters who take a break, possibly permanently, from trying to figure out what to do with each day.

"I am a continuer," Schlossberg said. She was reluctant to offer specific advice on when, whether, and how I should retire, but she was pretty sure about what category I fell into. "You will probably be a continuer and a searcher.... I think as someone who is engaged in writing and interviewing and critically looking at the world, you're not going to give all of that up. You don't know how it's all going to unfold, but I think people need to embrace ambiguity, because there is ambiguity and there is no quick answer."

All true, no doubt. But embracing ambiguity is what I've been doing for a few years now, unsure of whether it's time to make a change. I'm conflicted and ambiguous, maybe even stuck, and I'm eager to get past that. Of course I can't predict the future, but I'd like to have a better sense of what future I'm working toward, and I'm not there yet.

The more I talked to Schlossberg, the more I envied the way in which she found such purpose and relevance in her seventies, eighties, and nineties in designing a model for helping others through the transition. "Everything will change," she told me. "Your relationship with your wife, with your children, with your colleagues. Your daily routines will be changed and so will your assumptions about yourself and the world, and you need to have a map of what's in store.... Eventually you will establish a new life, but there will be ups and downs, a lot of questions and a lot of mixed emotions. This transition from an old life to a new life takes time."

When I mentioned that I had been wondering about whether I'd like to live reasonably close to my grown children in retirement, Schlossberg wouldn't offer either a guess or any advice. It would be more useful, she said, to understand that life, even in retirement and sometimes especially in retirement, is about dealing with the unexpected, with loss, with death, with altered relationships, with plans gone awry. When she lost her husband, she didn't expect what followed, namely, a fulfilling relationship with another man. When he died, after they were together for five years, she didn't know what might follow. But during our conversation, Schlossberg put me on hold briefly to take another call.

"I'm ninety-one and that was my boyfriend calling," she told me, chuckling over her embrace of life's endless possibilities.

NINE

T HE CALENDAR YEAR, POSSIBLY THE LAST YEAR OF FULL-
time employment in my life, is coming to a close. It's
Tuesday, December 29, at about 3:00 p.m., and my
phone is ringing.

I pick up and Mel Brooks says hello.

The Los Angeles I write about is the one that exists beyond
the entertainment industry. That Los Angeles is much like any
other big city where people try to find their way, scratching out
lives filled with small satisfactions and crushing disappoint-
ments. Teachers, social workers, problem solvers, thinkers,
barbershop owners, eccentrics, loners, wannabes, saints, and
sinners. But sometimes I hear from celebrities who respond
to a column I've written. I got to know Eva Marie Saint a little
bit because she and her husband, producer Jeff Hayden, responded to columns I wrote. I have not met two more gracious,
humble people in all of L.A. Jeff died five years ago, and Eva
Marie took it very hard. Jeff loved to garden, and one day, after
his death, I was visiting Eva Marie when she took me out to
her patio to show me a flower that had sprouted without a seed
being planted. It was the same type of flower Jeff used to plant

in that very box. Eva Marie was overjoyed by the unexpected bloom, as if it were a gift from Jeff.

Mel Brooks was on the line because I had reached out to him, just as I've reached out to dozens of retirement-age people from normal walks of life. I knew from reading about Brooks's various projects that the man doesn't seem to know how to retire. I wanted to know how a legend in his nineties keeps his edge and stays in the game.

"There's nothing about this guy that's retiring," Kevin Salter, who has worked on Mel Brooks's productions for many years, told me when he agreed to set up my interview. In 2012, Salter said that Brooks had told him, "I'm feeling a little bored right now in what I'm doing. I've done *The Producers* on Broadway, I've done *Young Frankenstein*, and I'm not creating any new content."

Salter suggested Brooks try an HBO special in which the writer, producer, actor, and comic told personal stories.

"We decided to take the act on the road, and for most of the last decade we crisscrossed the country, went to London and everywhere else and Mel did live events," Salter said. He told me that Brooks is still tinkering with different projects, and he certainly isn't sitting on the sofa wondering what to do with himself. He's currently working on his memoir and adapting his film *History of the World, Part I* into a series he will write, produce, and narrate.

I didn't know how much Salter had told Brooks about my book project, so I gave Brooks a quick primer. I'd seen something in the news about how Brooks still hadn't walked away from the work, in his nineties, which made me feel like a quitter for wondering how much gas I had left in the tank at a mere sixty-seven. Did retirement hold no appeal for Brooks? Did work keep him young? Did a creative force give him no choice but to keep going?

"I would tell you right now it's not heavy lifting," Brooks said. "It's not physical work, like working in a coal mine somewhere. It's just using your mind. All I need is my pencil."

Good point. Sure, finding stories and writing them can be taxing at times. But calling it work, especially when it's something you love, doesn't seem fair. Especially when you consider how many people have physically demanding, highly stressful, or monotonous work. Or work they hate. I do feel privileged to have the job I have, and I told Brooks I still get a lot out of it.

"Then keep doing it," he said. "Because if you don't, the devil will find ways to occupy your mind."

His voice was strong, his mind sharp. Pure luck, or do you lose fewer brain cells by always trying to find stories that haven't been told? A few years ago, I began having trouble remembering the names of people familiar to me as well as the names of television shows and athletes and of restaurants I'd been to. It scared the hell out of me because I had seen the same thing in both my parents when they were my age, and their cognitive decline was steady from that point on. A friend suggested I forget some things simply because there's a lot rattling around in my head as part of my job. This same person told me that forgetting is normal, throughout life, but that you become more aware of it when you're older, because you fear that forgetting is new and you'll never be the same. I don't know if there's any science behind that, but I hope it's true.

In my conversation with Brooks, a combat engineer who defused land mines as Allied forces rolled into the Battle of the Bulge during World War II, he didn't seem to have forgotten much of anything. He talked about his career, his friends, and even his regrets in a career so varied a lot of people probably don't know half of it. An uncle took him to a Broadway show when he was a kid, and Brooks proclaimed he wasn't going to work in the New York Garment District like so many other tenement dwellers. He was going to be in show business. Even if he believed that at the time, he couldn't have imagined the success he was in for. Brooks won an Oscar for best original screenplay for *The Producers*. He won an Emmy for writing a television special with Sid Caesar, Imogene Coca, and Carl Reiner. He won three best supporting actor Emmys for his work on *Mad About You*. He won three Tony Awards for *The Producers*—outstanding musical, outstanding original screenplay, and outstanding lyrics. He won two Grammys for *The Producers* and one for best comedy album for skits with Reiner that were called "The 2000-Year-Old Man," in which Reiner would ask Brooks what life was like back in the day.

"Sir," Reiner said in one skit, "do you remember the very first book you ever read?"

"I was a child," Brooks says. "It was a simple book in the ancient Hebrew." Brooks mutters three Yiddish-sounding words and says, "That translates into 'See Moses Run.' . . . It was a page-turner." Brooks went on to say he knew "the head writer" of the Bible. "He lived two caves away."[1]

All of it was ad-libbed, Brooks told me. He and Reiner worked together on a television variety show called *Your Show of Shows*, and they kept sampling new material. Brooks says he didn't know what Reiner was going to ask him, and Reiner didn't know how Brooks would respond. It all began, Reiner once said, like this:

"I turned to Mel and I said, 'Here's a man who was actually seen at the crucifixion 2,000 years ago,' and his first words were, 'Oh, boy.' We all fell over laughing. I said, 'You knew Jesus?' 'Yeah,' he said, 'Thin lad, wore sandals, long hair, walked around with 11 other guys. Always came into the store, never bought anything. Always asked for water.' Those were the first words, and then for the next hour or two I kept asking him questions, and he never stopped killing us."[2]

It was like a vaudeville act, and it was such a hit, six comedy albums and an animated television series resulted, and comedians for years said they'd been inspired by the offbeat wackiness of "The 2,000-Year-Old Man." And yet that's but a footnote in Brooks's long career, for which he was given the 2015 National Medal of Arts for lifetime achievement. But like anyone who lives a long life, Brooks has suffered a lot of heartbreak. He lost his good buddy Gene Wilder, whom he credited with introducing him to fine wine. "I was drinking Manischewitz," Brooks said, until Wilder tutored him. He lost Reiner, his longtime collaborator and buddy. And he lost the woman he was married to for forty years, Oscar-winning actress Anne Bancroft.

Brooks told me he regretted having become typecast as a funny man. "When you have great success as a comic, there's an expectation that you'll keep giving your fans more of the same," he said. It's not a bad occupational hazard to have, though, when your box office hits include *Blazing Saddles* (1974), *Young Frankenstein* (1974), *Silent Movie* (1976), *High Anxiety* (1977), and *Spaceballs* (1987).

"I just hated that idea," Brooks said. "What makes you breaks you. What does that mean? Well, when you're good at something, you do that. People ask you for that. They *plead* for that, to do that thing you do. And you say you're sick and tired of that shit, but meanwhile, you've perfected it."

Brooks helped make a lot of more serious and sober entertainment, but he said he was so concerned about audience expectations, he kept his coproducer credit off the 1980 drama *The Elephant Man*, which was nominated for eight Academy Awards, including best picture. "People would have seen my name and thought it was a comedy," Brooks said of the David Lynch–directed movie, in which a physically deformed man played by John Hurt ends up in a London freak show, sadistically exploited by his ringmaster. Brooks's production company, Brooksfilms, also churned out the dramas *Frances* (1982), *My Favorite Year* (1982), *The Fly* (1986), and *84 Charing Cross Road* (1987).

But some of Brooks's projects that were seen as farce were intended as social and political commentary, and *The Producers*, one of Brooks's crowning achievements, is the best example. The 1967 black comedy starred Zero Mostel and Gene Wilder, and it was followed twenty-four years later by a massive Broadway hit starring Nathan Lane and Matthew Broderick, with twelve Tony Awards, multiple overseas productions, and later a film based on the play, which opened with a musical number called "Springtime for Hitler." Brooks's creation was revolutionary for its send-up of Hitler and drew both critical acclaim and shocked indignation for its satirical treatment of one of the most diabolical madmen in human history.

"I didn't think I was sinful in any way," Brooks once told *Entertainment Weekly*. "I thought it was making a point: You get up on a soapbox and you argue with a Nazi, you're going to lose. But if you can ridicule him and make people laugh, then you win. It's as simple as that."[3]

All these years later, Brooks told me, he writes about five days a week. When he's not working on his memoir, he's working on

other projects "that I can't talk about right now." That's not uncommon in Hollywood, where creators don't want to give ideas
away or begin selling tickets before all the pieces come together.

"I was meant to tell stories and sometimes perform," Brooks
told me. "I'm still thinking. I'm lucky my brain still works."

If I wanted to talk to people who didn't know when to quit
working, Brooks said, I should get in touch with his friend
Norman Lloyd, who began acting in 1939 and kept at it until
2015. Brooks then described a scene from Alfred Hitchcock's
1942 movie, *Saboteur*, in which a character played by Lloyd
met a horrible fate after dangling from the tip of the Statue
of Liberty.

"He plays the bad guy and it's a great scene. Robert Cummings grabs him by the sleeve of his jacket, and even though
Lloyd's the bad guy, Cummings hangs onto him to save his
life. And then Hitchcock moves the camera down Lloyd's
sleeve to his armpit and keeps it there for a while and then
pop, pop, pop. The sleeve comes free and Norman Lloyd falls
and screams."

Okay, I thought. This is pretty cool. I'm interviewing Mel
Brooks, and he's raving about a Hitchcock scene. And I've only
gotten this chance because Brooks is familiar with my work as
a columnist.

"You're the Frank Capra of the *L.A. Times*, always telling
warm, heartfelt stories," Brooks tells me.

Well, not always, because I do knock people around at times.
I thank Brooks for the compliment, and I say that, just like him,
the work still matters to me. But we don't all know we're going
to last into our nineties, let alone live to two thousand. And I
might want to see what it's like to live in Spain for a while or on
a kibbutz or do something I haven't even thought of yet.

"Then do it," Brooks said. He told me I should go to my boss right away and ask if I could switch things up a little bit, work half-time, and try some other things the other half of the time.

"I'd say keep doing what you're doing, but don't do as much of it," Brooks said. "But always look forward to waking up with something that you do well. Something that you want to do."

TEN

ONE YEAR ENDS, ANOTHER BEGINS, AND THIS ONE WILL BE filled with milestones.

- I'm about to mark twenty years in my current job and forty-six as an ink-stained wretch.
- Alison will turn sixty.
- She and I will celebrate our twenty-fifth wedding anniversary.
- Caroline will turn eighteen, graduate from high school, and depart for college.
- And I may retire, possibly on the Fourth of July, because why shouldn't there be fireworks to mark the big day?

On New Year's Eve, reflecting on a year of ugly division in our country, a sense of weariness comes over me, and retirement doesn't seem like the worst idea I'd ever had. Maybe it's battle fatigue, a feeling that there is no longer much of a public service in telling stories, because our toxic culture has driven us into silos where we believe what we want to believe and an echo chamber affirms our every conviction, no matter how misguided.

I keep doing my job, which means leaving the house on reporting trips and interviewing people for columns, always at what I hope is a safe distance. But I'm not young, and my battery-operated implant prevents my electrically malfunctioning heart from shutting down, becoming as dead as a cold potato. With every irregular flutter, I'm all but certain of my imminent death. I emailed my cardiologist one day to ask if I fit the definition of preexisting conditions likely to doom my chance of survival if I contract COVID from inhaling a molecule of bad air or from not properly sanitizing a box of Cheez-Its and then touching my face. The cardiologist says no, I'm not likely to be in danger, so calm down, sit tight, and stop worrying.

Good advice from the doctor, and in countless ways I'm one of the lucky ones. Not only have I kept my job, but a temporary furlough that had been imposed to save money during the pandemic has been lifted, and I'm back to a five-day workweek. The markets continue to rebound, so unless there's another crash, which of course is entirely possible, I won't have to delay retirement to build the savings back up. The pandemic thrashing of Wall Street, by the way, sent shivers through me. Watching a modest nest egg, built up over fifty years, shrink before my eyes on the eve of what might be my retirement kept me up at night.

If I haven't already gotten this point across, I'm a coward when it comes to money, a commodity I don't really know much about. I live by one guiding principle: do not buy things you don't need with money you don't have. This has something to do with the fact that my parents were children of the Depression, which means they lived like farmers who never took the next harvest for granted. My mother spoke reverently about a neighbor who would drive twenty miles to save a penny on a gallon of gas. The neighbor was not a math major, obviously, but he was a person of unshakable principle. During my childhood, if we went out to dinner, it was never ever to a fancy place, and by fancy, I mean the kind of place where soup, salad, and a basket of bread are not included in the price of the entrée. Even at that, my mother would often look the menu over with a critical eye, wondering how they could possibly charge what they were charging for, say, meatloaf or chicken fried steak, then gaze up at the waiter and say, "I'll just have water." But my father was the king of austere living. If something broke—a clock, a washing machine, a shovel— he jerry-rigged a fix. In the days when air-conditioning was available on any new vehicle, we were out of luck, because we never bought new vehicles. But we did have a portable air conditioner in our used car that sat on peg legs between the driver and front-seat passenger. It looked like something from *Gilligan's Island*. Water dripped through a wall of straw, and a fan pushed bad air into the car, giving all of us hay fever for life. If one of my dad's used beaters broke down on the highway, did he call a tow truck? He did not. He called Uncle Mike, who gladly raced to our aid with ropes and chains and towed us to where another friend or relative would tinker under the hood. And when the tires were as bald as bowl- ing balls, my father bought recaps. Have you ever heard of them? You go to a tire shop that cannibalizes parts from junk- yards, and the repairman slices some halfway decent tread off another tire and hot-glues it onto your tire. Then you drive away, fingers crossed, hoping the recaps don't shred like con- fetti at sixty miles an hour. So it's probably not surprising that the last three vehicles I have purchased were all used or that I was sick to my stomach watching the pandemic burn through our retirement fund. Thank God I didn't freeze all our assets, because I would have missed the rebound.

But again, I'm one of the lucky ones. A study by the National Institute on Retirement Security finds that 51 percent of Americans surveyed fear they won't be able to retire with a stable income, 33 percent are rethinking retirement, and more than two-thirds say they now plan to retire later due to lost hours, diminished pay, furloughs, and layoffs.[1]

And then there are those who have a pretty good strategy for avoiding financial hardship in retirement. They will just keep working. I saw a headline about one such person: "An 80-year-old doctor on why he refuses to retire anytime soon—'I plan to die in the office.'" The author was Richard Besdine, a geriatrician who studies longevity.[2]

"At 80 years old, I still wake up and go to work every day. I'm a geriatrician—and it's a job that I've held for the past 55 years," wrote Besdine, a professor of Medicine and Health Services Policy at Brown University and a former president of the American Geriatrics Society.

"The average retirement age in the U.S. [is] around 64. I'm way past that, but I don't plan on retiring anytime soon. Why? For starters, I happen to be among the lucky few who love the work they do. (I know I'm in the minority with this, so I do feel extremely grateful.)"

I called Besdine and told him one of my fears is anchored in the experiences of my parents, both of whom had dementia that began in their sixties and seventies and grew much worse in their eighties. My thinking, because of that, is that maybe I should retire while I still have my wits about me and can enjoy doing something other than work.

"For us men," Besdine said, "most of our social ID is work-related. Even women who are CEOs have much richer social lives than men. We're stupid, you know? We screw it up time after time. When there's an opportunity to do the smart thing or the dumb thing, men do the dumb thing, from bungee jumping to neglecting a health screening."

Retiring for the sake of retiring can be one of those things, Besdine said. People who retire "to sleep late, stay in their pajamas all day, and start cocktails at three thirty instead of seven—those people go rather rapidly to hell in a handbasket."

All right, so I promise not to do that more than once or twice a week. If I'm going to hell either way, I'd like to take the long route.

"The most successful retirees," Besdine said, "either retire because they want to learn to fly an airplane or they feel they can be useful in some other way. But whatever it is, it has to be something that gets you out of bed in the morning."

Besdine told me he doesn't literally have a desire to die in his office but to continue doing what gives him relevance, in his case, studying, researching aging, and occasionally writing about health and the benefits of engagement. The older he gets, the more expert he becomes. And to keep his edge, he plays squash and eats a Mediterranean diet.

"I don't think there's anything I'm doing that I want to give up. Now what will change that? I don't think that if I discover knitting or rug making or learning to fly an airplane or learning to speak German, that any of that is going to supersede what I'm doing now. If I thought that what I was doing now was going to shorten my life span, I might have second thoughts. But, if anything, it's prolonging my life span in the sense that, if I stopped doing it, I'm not sure how I'll be."

I thought I'd take one last stab at justifying retirement by telling the doctor he was making perfect sense, and yet my business is rapidly changing in ways I don't necessarily find pleasing or acceptable. Dr. Besdine politely scoffed, saying that the world of medicine is changing, too, but that only makes him all the more determined to show up to work, practice his craft by the principles he's always believed in, and hope he can make a difference in the lives of others, if not the medical industry itself.

I'm losing track of the number of working people my age or older who are so virtuously committed to their passions, they make me feel lazy, uncommitted, or inadequate. But they are not the whole story here, and they are not my only guides. My retired tennis-playing buddies are all enjoying life and doing things I don't have the time to do. And then there's Mel Brooks and his argument for the hybrid model: you work a little, you play a little. Best of both worlds.

It's January 1, and the calendar says I am halfway to my self-imposed goal of figuring out what to do with the rest of my life, but I still feel as though anything is possible. And there's a rumor I need to check out. I hear that the *L.A. Times* may soon be offering buyout packages, which are, by design, more attractive to old-timers such as me. It's one more reason to leap, to say goodbye to one thing and hello to another. To sign my declaration of independence in this year of milestones.

ELEVEN

THE EMAIL ARRIVES AT 10:47 P.M. ON JANUARY 7. ALISON and I are ready to call it a night, and I know this is a bad habit, but I often make one last email check to see if there's anything I need to jump on early the next day. The email is from a retired county official, and he is passing along some news. Some really awful news.

> I was just notified that former City Councilman Tom LaBonge passed away this evening. Waiting for more details. Devastating news. Engine 35 responded to a cardiac arrest call at his home this evening.

I have to read it again. Tom LaBonge, dead? We were born nine days apart in October 1953, and he was healthy enough to begin every day with a sunrise hike on the slopes of Griffith Park in Los Angeles. The one time I joined him on that trek, I had trouble keeping up with LaBonge, who charged the slopes like a mountain goat.

Tom LaBonge, dead?

He hadn't even been retired for five years, after decades in public service. And now he was gone?

We were neighbors for many years. He was my councilman. His daughter was Caroline's babysitter. His wife, Brigid, is one of Alison's closest friends. I make a point not to become too closely engaged with any public official, because it's important in my business to maintain a professional rather than personal relationship. But I had written about LaBonge and gone to dinner with him, and I had cruised the city with him—one of his favorite things to do—as he visited all his favorite haunts and told stories about places, people, history. He called me periodically with column ideas while he was in office and afterward too. He always had somebody I needed to meet or a place I needed to visit, and he was always ready to hook up. I worried about how he'd be in retirement, because the job was so much a part of his identity. More than once, I asked what the next chapter would be, and he had a couple of possibilities in mind, but nothing had worked out for him yet. No doubt, there were headaches associated with being a councilman, and like any other politician, LaBonge had supporters and critics. But his job was a platform for serving people and for promoting the city, and I worried that the man whose name began, appropriately enough, with L and A, would ever be able to fill the void when he left office.

I know I have to tell Alison about the email I've just received, but I hesitate for an instant, knowing what a blow this will be to her. Alison and Brigid's friendship was centered, initially, around the fact that they were both volunteers at the public elementary school our kids had attended. They had both served as the equivalent of PTA president, and the friendship grew from there. It's late, and there's nothing we can do about the news, and I wonder if it would be better to wait and tell Alison in the morning. But it's a fleeting consideration.

"Tom LaBonge just died," I tell her.

She gasps. I hand her my phone.

Tears streaming, Alison jumps out of bed. Tom and Brigid both have big families, and their son, Charles, and daughter, Mary-Cate, are adults. We wonder if a phone call now would be an intrusion on the family in its worst moment. But Alison and Brigid are too close for Alison not to call and offer whatever support she can. She dials, and Brigid is in the first moments of a life forever transformed. She says she'd been downstairs in their house, went upstairs, and found Tom unconscious in the living room in front of the television. She called 911 but knew he was already gone. Brigid asks Alison to come to the house, so my wife hurriedly begins getting dressed. Caroline hears the commotion and comes to see what's going on. She, too, is rattled by the news. "Apparently," I tell Caroline, "it was cardiac arrest." She knows what that is and knows I had my own close call after my first knee surgery. I tell Alison I'm going to go with her, so she doesn't have to be alone. Caroline insists on joining us.

The ride to the LaBonge home takes about twenty minutes and we go in two cars, in case Alison needs to stay through the night. If there was anything Tom loved more than the city he served, it was his family. A family that often had to share him with constituents who needed help with this or that. He personally dragged bulky trash to the curb and helped toss it into dump trucks. If uplifted tree roots buckled your sidewalk or a traffic light wasn't working properly, Tom was there. We once had a power outage that lasted a couple of days in the middle of a wretched summer heat wave. I popped outside when the lights first dimmed to see if any neighbors were having the same problem, and Tom was at my corner, talking to a crew from the Department of Water and Power. He knew what the problem was (decaying power-line infrastructure overloaded by thousands of air conditioners running full force), and he knew which manhole covers the crew needed to check under. In a sprawling city of four million, Tom made you feel like you were living in a small town. He went to the neighborhood elementary school. He knew the house on my block that Judy Garland had grown up in, and he knew that she and Mickey Rooney used to walk up Ivanhoe Street together when they were kids. He cut ribbons, troubleshot problems at parks and rec centers, understood L.A.'s reservoir and water delivery systems better than anyone. I knew from our conversations that, in retirement, his daily routines weren't all that much of a departure from his days in public office. But he also had more time to devote to family, at least in theory if not in practice, and his death seemed all the more cruel because of it.

When we get to the house, several police officers and vehicles are out front. Alison goes inside and texts me and Caroline to say she hugged Brigid, who appeared to be in shock, unable to entirely accept that this was real. Alison tells us that there are quite a few people in the house, including police officers, and we should probably wait outside for her. She goes out to the back porch, where she and Brigid had often sipped wine and admired the spectacular view of the park Tom loved. Brigid and her daughter and son stay inside, near Tom's body, as they wait for the hearse. Alison would say later that another close friend, Mary Fran, joined her on the back porch, along with L.A. mayor Eric Garcetti. He had been one of the first people to show up at the house, and he was telling stories about Tom's commitment to duty, about his zeal for the job and for the city.

I wait in the car for a while, then get out to stretch my legs, strolling past police officers who are monitoring the comings and goings. A detective arrives and is briefed by the officers. An owl hoots, a cat jumps over a fence, shadows fall on solemn faces. I think back on the fun Tom and I had on a recent trip to Musso & Frank in the heart of Hollywood, where Tom knew all the tuxedoed waiters, one of whom gave him VIP attention and a big red booth at the end of the bar. I'm wishing we'd done that more often. I'm thinking about Tom's telling me we should go to L.A.'s sister city of Berlin together so he could show me around. And I'm thinking, for the first time since I began contemplating retirement, that maybe now I have my answer. One might argue that retirement, to a degree, had been Tom's undoing. And yet the more persuasive evidence before me on this horrible night in January is that our fragility is a constant, our plans go unrealized, our dreams vanish without warning, and there are no do overs.

Several hours before LaBonge died, another famous local Tom died at the age of ninety-three. Tommy Lasorda, the L.A. Dodgers former manager, a Hall of Famer, had been sick for a while, so there was no element of surprise as there had been with LaBonge. But it was not easy to imagine Los Angeles without those two Toms who had been so much a part of the city's essence. I call Garcetti the next day to talk about it for a column about the city's double loss.

"Tom LaBonge was the heart of L.A., and Tommy Lasorda was the soul of L.A.," Garcetti says. He notes that LaBonge loved the people of Los Angeles as much as he loved the city. When he met someone, he asked them what high school they attended, because, for him, it was a way of connecting. LaBonge was "someone who just loved everybody," Garcetti says, and

Lasorda was a fighter and competitor whose spirit was made of "grit and determination."

Garcetti had been on those car rides with LaBonge, Tom at the wheel of his big Crown Victoria, breezing under the palms as if Randy Newman's "I Love L.A." was on an endless reel in his head.

"It was like Mr. Toad's Wild Ride," Garcetti says.

"The day he died," the mayor goes on, "he was bringing water to workers next door, moving cars to help construction trucks get in place, and it was his favorite day of the week: trash day. So he was moving his neighbors' trash bins in and out."

Tom, who played football at John Marshall High, often carried a football with him on his daily rounds. He liked to tell stories about his teammate Andy Reid, who went on to coach the Kansas City Chiefs to a Super Bowl victory. The day I hiked Griffith Park with Tom, he tossed me the ball when we got to the top of Mount Hollywood.

Don't drop it, I thought. He'd caught me off guard and the ball was flying at me before I could set myself, but I didn't want to blow it.

"Touchdown!" Tom yelled when I pulled it in, his arms thrust skyward.

Godspeed, Mr. L.A.

TWELVE

I SELDOM MAKE NEW YEAR'S RESOLUTIONS BECAUSE, BY their very nature, they have a temporary quality to them. Anybody can find the motivation to end bad habits and start good ones on January 1, but the feeling of grandiosity quickly fades, because the suffering is real. Go ahead, give up chocolate. Congratulations. Let's see how long that lasts.

But this year is going to be different, or so I'm telling myself. If my retirement is coming up soon, I want to be in good enough shape to enjoy it. Even before Tom LaBonge died, I had decided to lose weight after a stressful year of lockdowns and lack of discipline added twenty pounds I didn't need. Slimming down would be easier on my knees and back (which ache all the time) and my heart. It'd be nice to get so fit that I might be able to quit the blood pressure capsules I pop every morning. And I'm long overdue for cleaner living after months of too much eating and too little movement. If I'd had more willpower I would have started before the holidays, but I didn't want to be overly depressed during a festive time. The new year has begun, though, and LaBonge's death has me thinking I'm on borrowed time from here on out, so maybe I need to juice my odds a little bit.

Do you know what George Washington, Leonardo da Vinci, Catherine the Great, Ingrid Bergman, Joe Frazier, Spencer Tracy, Johnnie Cochran, Peter Jennings, and Liberace have in common? They all died at age sixty-seven, and most people probably don't think of them as having died prematurely. So I'm in that zone now where people might generously say, "Wow, he died too young," but they're secretly thinking every day is a blessing once you enter senior citizen status.

Mobster Sam "Momo" Giancana died at sixty-seven, too, although nobody would call his death premature, given his line of work. Per accounts, Giancana was in the basement of his home in Oak Park, Illinois, on the night of June 19, 1975, cooking himself some sausage and peppers. Who cooks in the basement, you ask? Maybe somebody who doesn't want to be spotted through an upstairs kitchen window. Giancana had just had a gallbladder operation a week earlier, and doctors say you shouldn't have greasy or fatty foods after that particular surgery. But it wasn't the sausage that killed Sam. And it wasn't that he busted a seam from his gallbladder surgery. What killed Giancana was the spray of bullets fired into his head and neck from short range by a gunman with a .22 caliber pistol who somehow entered his home and followed the scent of the simmering sausage. Nobody was ever arrested, and theories abound, including one suggesting Giancana was sent to the big trunk in the sky because he was about to testify about the Mafia hooking up with the CIA in a plot to assassinate Fidel Castro. Whatever the truth, Giancana is a good example of a guy who should have retired young, before he made so many enemies, and sometimes when I read my hate mail, I feel the same way.

I'm not in the Mafia, but I do eat sausage and peppers, and I'm not going to stop now. And my weight-loss strategy doesn't require me to. Notice that I used the words *weight-loss strategy* rather than diet. That's because diets don't work. If they worked, the weight-loss market wouldn't have beefed up to a record $78 billion in 2019, even as the percentage of obese Americans ballooned.[1] I speak from experience, having tried one or two fad diets over the years. You buy in, literally, and get hooked when the weight starts coming off, two pounds one week, three pounds the next. You feel great and can't believe you didn't start sooner. But then, right around the time a week of sacrifice barely registers on the scale, you notice that the packaged meal bars you've been eating—the ones you originally thought you liked—actually taste like potting soil. Here you are now with no bread, no cereal, no pasta, no potatoes. And you've had to cut way back on the alcohol, which is the very thing you need to get through the misery. That's how these diets work. First they take away simple pleasures. Then they take away your will to live.

Speaking of Tommy Lasorda, do you remember those television commercials in the 1990s when he was a spokesman for Ultra SlimFast? They began with a photo of Lasorda as a proudly pudgy manager for the Dodgers.

"When I looked like this, my guys challenged me to lose twenty pounds. Me, Tommy Lasorda. The guy who loves to eat. Well, I lost thirty pounds in three months with Ultra SlimFast," says Lasorda.

In another spot, beginning with the same pre-diet photo of the Dodger skipper, Lasorda says, "A year ago, when I looked like this, you'd never catch me in a bathing suit. But that was before I lost thirty pounds in three months with Ultra SlimFast."[2]

The commercials were undeniably compelling. I remember doing it Tommy's way in the nineties, walking over to the Wawa market in my Philadelphia neighborhood and buying a can of SlimFast for breakfast or lunch, then eating a normal meal for dinner, just like Tommy. It helped, but come on, I was living in Philadelphia. When half the city is at the Reading Terminal Market in the morning and ordering a breakfast of scrapple, runny eggs, and griddled hash browns at the Amish diner, it's tough to keep reaching for a can of liquid chalk. Then it's lunchtime, and you can't go three blocks without coming upon the scent of beef and onions sizzling on a grill. If they'd had cheese steak–flavored SlimFast in Philadelphia, I might have had a chance. But Tommy's weight-loss plan didn't work for me, and in the long run, it didn't work for Tommy. That's because diets are hard to stick with, no matter how sanctimonious and self-satisfied the practitioners are, and they are pretty much always sanctimonious and self-satisfied, until you don't see them for a few months and then, when you do, they're bigger than they were to begin with.

Twenty-five years after those SlimFast commercials, in the year 2014, a Dodgers PR guy pitched me a column on Dave Pearson, a Dodger Stadium chef for more than forty years. Pearson had been assigned to the press box for a decade, serving up pregame meals to Dodger announcers, bigwigs, and Hall of Famers. One of the regulars at Dave's Diner was Lasorda. In my several hours at the stadium, I saw Lasorda eat a burrito, followed by a ham and Swiss sandwich the size of a catcher's mitt. For dessert, he scraped clean a big bowl of mint chocolate-chip ice cream, and then for dinner, he dug into a heaping plate of Pearson's lasagna.

"Outstanding," said Lasorda, who told me the only person in the world who cooked better Italian food than Dave Pearson was Lasorda's mother.

SlimFast was ancient history with Lasorda, and for good reason. As I was saying, diets don't last. That's why I came up with my own weight-loss program, although Alison keeps insisting she deserves full credit for the idea. Over the years, when I told her I was thinking about starting the Paleo or the Keto or any other fad diet, she would give me an eye roll followed by one of her withering looks, and then she'd say something along the line of "Are you entirely clueless?"

Yes, but what's that got to do with it?

"Instead of denying yourself life's simple pleasures," she'd ask, "why not try moderation? And why not get your ass off the couch more often?"

The answer is that it's no fun to tell people you're experimenting with moderation. You can't get sanctimonious about it, and there are no television commercials extolling the virtues of scaling back just a bit. There's no product to sell and no buy-in from the delusional masses. But I'm here to tell you that I am on a two-step moderation plan as I write. First, I eat and drink a little bit less. Second, I exercise a little bit more.

That's it. There's no browsing the aisles of supermarkets for Keto products. There's no denying myself the occasional French fry or plate of pasta, and if I have a craving for pancakes, I'm going to reach for the original Bisquick, by Betty Crocker, not some box of almond dust that fills my plate but is guaranteed to disappoint. What I am going to do is use a little less butter, maybe substitute fresh fruit for syrup, and eat just a pancake or two instead of a stack. You can call it a diet if you want. But I'm thinking of it as sensible eating.

The pounds come off relatively easily at first, or so I try to convince myself. By mid-January I've dropped from 220 to 215. It's working, and I haven't said no to a sandwich or a ravioli or a side of mashed potatoes. Not that there hasn't been some sacrifice. I've stopped eating junk. No chips, no salty crackers, no snacks between meals unless it's fruit or nuts. And three nights a week, no alcohol at all. That's been the hardest part so far, be-cause I had allowed the pandemic to be my excuse for drinking beer or wine or a couple of shots of vodka or bourbon, or all of the above, just about every night of the week. You know, to take the edge off the pain of the shutdown. So less alcohol, smaller portions, no junk, and then there's the exercise part of the deal.

For the longest time, I've exercised for thirty minutes a day, either swimming laps or riding a stationary bike. Until tennis courts were closed, I played tennis with Alison once or twice a week for an hour or an hour and a half. On the new plan, I've added a daily walk of thirty to forty-five minutes, usually with my dog, Dominic, who also appears to be losing weight. When I have time, I drive over to the Rose Bowl, which is ten minutes from my house, and walk around the perimeter of the football stadium, the adjacent golf course, and the playing fields. That's about a three-mile walk, which takes me about fifty minutes, after which I either swim or ride the bike for half an hour.

I've got two months and two weeks to drop another fifteen pounds, and I'm determined not to backslide.

And if I lose a total of twenty pounds, then what?

This is a lifestyle, not a diet, so more moderation, I guess, regardless of whether I keep working or retire.

And not a drop of SlimFast.

THIRTEEN

THE OLDER YOU GET, THE MORE REMARKABLE YOU FIND old people. You think, "Look at them. Still here. Could that be me?" As I catch up to these people, I want to know them better. This is essentially a book about aging as much as it's about retirement. What are the secrets of aging well? I've been taking notes.

Hedda Bolgar, a therapist, worked until she was 102. In 2013, she was called to Washington, DC, where she and a 101-year-old custodian at a Maryland post office were named Outstanding Oldest Workers of the year. Bolgar told me at the time that she was beginning to worry about the ethics of still seeing clients who might not be able to lean on her much longer. But she was sharp and still had something to give.

"What I grew up with was, if there's an unmet need in the world, you try to meet it, and if there's a problem, you try to solve it," Hedda told me.

She said she had a client in his eighties who woke up each day wishing he would die, and he wanted to know her magic for celebrating every day of life.

"I tell him there is no magic and he cannot accept it," Hedda told me. "He cannot accept that he's old."

Bolgar, who fled Europe when Germany annexed Austria, was still hosting salons at her home in Los Angeles in her final years, bringing great minds together to share ideas about the issues of the day. She was still involved with an institute she cofounded to counsel people who could not afford therapists. And she told me she still had much to accomplish.

"I'm too busy to die," she said in an airy, sunlit room of her house. Through the windows, color exploded in a flower garden that looked like it should be in a magazine.

Hedda made it to 103.

———

May Lee works in general accounting for the state of California, studying the operating budgets of dozens of state government buildings to make sure no mistakes are being made with taxpayer money.

Nothing about that is particularly noteworthy. It's a relatively anonymous, routine job in a big bureaucracy.

But there's something a little different about May.

For starters, she began her job in 1943.

A gallon of gas cost fifteen cents, the president was Franklin D. Roosevelt, the Germans suffered defeat at Stalingrad.

May actually started in the state finance department and moved in 1963 to general accounting. Last summer, she turned one hundred and celebrated her seventy-seventh year on the job.

"I like to work with numbers," May told me when I asked why she's still at it. "I like to balance things."

Her one regret is that, when the pandemic hit, she had to work from home. Gone, at least temporarily, was the joy of driving herself to work in her Ford Escort and enjoying the company of colleagues.

May has worked for ten governors. She was one of the first Chinese American employees in state government, and she argued in testimony before the legislature that it was time to end a shameful policy of discrimination and hire more people like her. May used an abacus when she started, still prefers a pencil and adding machine to a computer, and has been credited with saving taxpayers tens of millions of dollars over the years by spotting accounting errors.

I learned about May when the state issued a press release about her years of service, and I found a television news clip about the event.

"She is vital to this department. She has taught and mentored a lot of us," said a coworker, who didn't say so for the sake of being generous.

"Most people would look at her and say she should maybe be in a rocking chair on a porch somewhere, but she's still coming and contributing," said a supervisor.

May lives with a niece, Laurel Lee, who retired from the Air Force a few years ago.

"I gave her a hard time, because she promised she would consider retiring when I did," Laurel told me.

May told me she actually thought about retiring many years ago, because she'd reached the point where she'd make about as much from retirement pay as she did on the job. But she couldn't think of anything she'd rather do than go to work, where she feels appreciated and valued. Technically, she is what's called a retired annuitant, which means she can work up to 960 hours a year for pay. But rumor has it that May works many more hours than that, essentially volunteering.

When I asked May about her life, she said she has no regrets about anything. She traveled quite a bit when she was younger, she told me, visiting just about every corner of the world. But she uses a walker now, and traveling doesn't appeal as much as it used to.

What appeals is the work that began seventy-seven years ago and is never finished. The state had five buildings when she started her career and more than sixty today. Laurel assured me that if any of those buildings have any operating budget errors, May is going to find them.

When she's not working, May loves to read. When I spoke with her, she was halfway through a book on the real-life Chinese immigrant detective who was fictionalized as Charlie Chan.

Any secrets to a long life?

May said she eats a lot of fruit and vegetables and a little bit of meat. Nothing fried. But there's more to it than that.

"Be positive and make people happy," she told me, and she had one more piece of advice.

Do what you love to do.

—⁂—

When I began this project last July, I reached out to Morrie Markoff, who was 105 at the time. I had known him for six years, beginning with an email he sent me. He had just read my column about my flatlining in the hospital, and he wrote to say, "Welcome to the club." The same thing had happened to him when he was hospitalized with a heart issue, Morrie said, and his family thought he was a goner. The only thing different in his case was that it happened a bit later in life. He died the day before he turned ninety-nine. Morrie wanted to know if I wanted to get together for a cup of coffee, now that we were both members of the Back from the Dead Club.

In the years since, I've been to Morrie's one hundredth birthday party and to his seventy-fifth wedding anniversary. He lost Betty, the love of his life, in September 2019. He was holding her hand at the time. She was 103. Morrie, a bit of a revolutionary in his day, wrote a love letter to his departed wife, whom he referred to as both Betty and Betsy.

"I won't forget you twice being arrested for leafletting for civil rights and always standing up against injustice," Morrie wrote. "Betsy doll, wherever you are, in the heavens or on a star, that's where I want to be with you. For 80 years I've held your hand, our fingers tightly enjoined. Betsy doll, I love you."

Morrie and Betty used to ride buses together to explore the city. One day he told me he'd met an interesting woman on the bus who owned an art gallery in Chinatown. They got to talking, and Morrie told her he used to own an appliance repair shop in Los Angeles, and when business was slow, he made sculpture out of scrap metal. It all started when he spotted a used toilet float in the shop and noticed that it looked like the skirt of a ballerina. So Morrie went to work and made a sculpture of a ballerina. It was the beginning of an obsession, and Morrie went on to make dozens of pieces, drawing on a lifetime of inspiration. The guys he played chess with in the park. His daughter reading a book. Construction workers raising a building. Morrie still had the sculptures, decades later, on shelves and in closets. The gallery owner he met on the bus, Tracy Huston of the Red Pipe Gallery, was curious enough to ask Morrie if she could see his work. "Sure," said Morrie, "come on over."

"It was an extraordinary delight," Huston told me. "The execution and craft are fantastic, and he also created what is his own style."

At the age of one hundred, Morrie had his first art show. His blue eyes twinkled as he greeted fans at the Red Pipe gallery.

And he wasn't done reinventing himself. For at least a couple of years, Morrie would update me on his first book, a memoir. He worked on it day and night, determined to share with the world what he had learned in his century-long life.

The book was published when Morrie was 102, and he titled it after the answer he gave to people who asked him the secret of a long life: *Keep Breathing*.[1]

Morrie had a booth at the *Los Angeles Times* Festival of Books and signed copies of his memoir, and when that was done, he immediately started writing a sequel.

That's the Morrie I know, and when I told him I was thinking about retiring and wanted to pick his brain, Morrie told me he wanted to collect his thoughts on paper and mail me a letter.

A couple of weeks later, I received an envelope that contained three letters from Morrie, each written in longhand cursive on lined paper.

"I came to Los Angeles driving an old battered 1928 Ford," the New York native wrote. "I reached Nirvana, a land of orange blossoms and heavenly smells, in 10 days. The year was 1931, the very heart of the Depression. . . . Too much to tell. Come see me."

I wanted to but couldn't. Morrie had just been whisked away from a senior living facility where several people had died of COVID-19. He was staying in a downtown Los Angeles apartment with his caretaker, and neither of us could risk a get-together at the height of the pandemic. In the second letter,

Morrie reminded me that he was "one of the oldest geezers around."

> I say it's not the length of life that matters but how you live it. When all is said and done I lived a long and fulfilling one. I am a lucky man. Wonderful wife, we had 80 years together. We traveled the world. Children and grandchildren we are proud of and love. We had many friends and many good times together. Question. Would I like another go around? Answer... No. I don't want to push my luck. Adios. And good luck to you.

In the third letter, Morrie told me he was troubled by the police killing of a black man—George Floyd—in Minneapolis and what it said about race relations in the United States more than half a century after the assassination of Martin Luther King Jr. In the middle of the night, Morrie got out of bed to write about what he had been witnessing on television, with protests across the land. His caretaker was alarmed, though not entirely surprised.

"Morrie, what are you doing up? It's four in the morning. Go to bed. You can write in the morning," Danny the caretaker told him.

But Morrie couldn't wait. He had to process his thoughts. He had to get them down on paper before the sun came up, in longhand cursive, because Morrie is retired from work but not from life.

As I write, Morrie is 106.

FOURTEEN

Yes, Morrie is a lucky soul. So is May Lee and so was Hedda Bolgar. Few of us can expect to be of reasonably sound mind and body that late in life or to have the energy to do much of anything, let alone keep learning and yearning. But what if I'm one of the lucky ones and live into my eighties or nineties? Will I still have the same level of curiosity, the same need for creative expression that are so much a part of who I am today? And will I still want to work in some fashion or another? I've been fond of Morrie Markoff since the day I met him, but never was I more inspired than by his story about rising before the sun because a thought, an outrage over an injustice, was bubbling up and he had to get to work, put pen to paper, and process a moment in history. If that's how I live my final years, dragged out of bed by the urge to write, I'll consider my life a success.

Another lucky guy, in this regard, is Norman Lear. When I first reached out to Mel Brooks, I also put in a request to speak to Lear, who is still working at ninety-eight. "I'd like to speak to him about creativity as a life force, and whether we can survive without honoring it," I wrote in an emailed request for an interview. One reason I wanted to talk to Lear was that, in his speeches, essays, and interviews, it was clear he'd given a lot of thought to meaning, identity, purpose, and life as a spiritual journey. He once told an interviewer who asked how he kept a sharp mind: "I haven't stopped learning about myself and my life. I think the vertical journey into oneself never ends."[1] In a 2016 interview with Oprah Winfrey, he said of his search for meaning, "I'm still at it. Because I don't really know, I grope. Along a thousand miles of river, the climate changes. As a result of the climate changing, the vegetation changes. But the water that nurtures it all, the spiritual water, nourishes everything. So that's the way I feel about the life of the spirit."[2]

My request was passed along with no guarantees because, for one thing, Lear is hard at work and extremely busy. In his autobiography, *Even This I Get to Experience*,[3] he quoted his mother's response when, in 1949, he said he was pining to leave Connecticut for California and a career in public relations.

"Hollywood's not for you, dear," his mother said.

No, not much. For seventy years, Lear has been one of the most prolific writers and producers in entertainment history. His hit shows include the groundbreaking *All in the Family*, *Sanford and Son*, *The Jeffersons,* and *Maude*. He's won four Emmys, two Peabody Awards, and the National Medal of Arts, and he's produced several hit movies, including *Stand by Me* and *The Princess Bride*. His political activism—rooted in a lefty, soul-searching spirituality and belief in the idea that we are all versions of each other—has been as extensive as his creative work, and it's almost sinful of me to represent it in shorthand. But here goes. Lear has celebrated and advocated for the protection of the First Amendment, he has campaigned against the influence of religious dogma in government and culture, and he once purchased a copy of the Declaration of Independence and toured the country to celebrate American history and civic engagement. He also, as a young man, flew fifty-two combat missions over Europe as a radio operator and gunner during World War II.

I finally received word that Lear had said yes to an interview, but he wanted to Zoom rather than meet in person. That was fine by me, and I got a preview of what it would be like to chat with him ten days before our scheduled meeting when Lear appeared on *CBS Sunday Morning* to mark the fiftieth anniversary of the premiere of *All in the Family*. The reporter was Lear's son-in-law, CBS News chief medical correspondent Jonathan LaPook, a physician, and the title of the piece was "What Makes Norman Lear, at 98, Still Tick?"[4]

"I have six children and four grandchildren," Lear said. "They all make me tick."

Lear said laughter is good medicine if you want to hang around awhile. "I happen to believe it has everything to do with a long and healthy life." He talked, too, about a belief that every man is his superior, because there are things he can learn from others. His long pen-pal relationship with President Ronald Reagan was mentioned, with Lear explaining it's worth hearing the perspectives of those with whom you have political differences, an idea that couldn't be more relevant today. And he said he still enjoys work.

"I am hungry to go to the office. I hunger to see the people I work with. I mean, there's no business like show business," Lear said.

His wife, Lyn Davis Lear, said she had asked him to slow down, but she knew the futility of her counsel. Lear continues to produce shows and pitch new ones to the networks.

"He's not the retiring type," Lyn said. "He loves that office and he's got, what, six shows possibly coming up? I mean it's just crazy."

The last topic of the CBS piece was death.

"I don't mind the going," Lear told his son-in-law. "It's the leaving that is the problem. Going, who knows what's out there? It can't be all bad. But leaving—I can't think of anything good about leaving."

Soon enough, I have my own chance to pick Lear's brain. A little after 10:00 a.m. on the scheduled day, a bespectacled Lear pops up on my computer screen. His signature white bucket hat tops a round, elfin face, making him seem all the more Yoda-like, and a warmth appears to have settled in permanently around his eyes. I'd been told he was on a tight schedule, so I jump right in, reminding him that I'm thinking about retiring. The whole point, of course, is to tunnel into the mind of a man who has thirty-one years on me and is still in the saddle, motivated perhaps by creative energy. But as the words about retirement come out of my mouth, I feel weak and a little foolish.

Has Lear *ever* thought about retiring?

"Never for a second," he says, and I feel even more impotent.

"I'm surprised to hear myself say I've never really thought about retirement," Lear tells me, thinking out loud. "I don't feel any awe about that. But usually, when I go to sleep at night, I have something that I'm thinking. Among other things, it's about something I'm doing tomorrow ... a day in which there are things I wish to do. So today is over, and we're on to the next."

That idea, I knew, was central to Lear's philosophy of life. In speeches and interviews, he returns frequently to the notion that human existence is a series of transitions from what has been completed to what's next on the agenda.

"If there were a hammock between those two words, *over* and *next*," Lear tells me, "that's the best way I know of living in the moment.... So long as I am interested in the next, I'm moving. And there have been, for ninety-eight years, a lot of wonderful nexts."

I'm not privy to the particulars of Lear's financial situation, but I think it's safe to assume he's in pretty good shape after three-quarters of a century of epic critical acclaim and commercial success. So it's not like he's juggling six show pitches, as his wife said on CBS, because he's having trouble paying the bills. He's somebody who works for the love of the labor, and there's actual labor involved. Lear tells me writing doesn't come easily to him early on in the birthing process, as he tries to give shape to an idea. He sets the bar high. A television show has to meet his standards for both entertainment value and social commentary. In a 2015 speech at the John F. Kennedy Center for the Performing Arts, Lear said this about why he produced programs that addressed real issues that were not being addressed on other shows:

> Some families were poor, some impoverished, bigotry was alive and well, some people cursed, women suffered menopause, men fought impotence, and the question of abortion was a topic of discussion in homes everywhere. Nothing we touched on was foreign to our viewers. And yet, script after script, we were told, "You can't do it, it won't fly in Des Moines," or, "There'll be a knee-jerk reaction in the Bible Belt. You can't go there." We went there. And not a single state seceded from the Union. As I said, we were accused of sending messages. If making bigotry sound foolish is a message, we stand guilty, I responded. And then one day I thought about the shows that preceded our arrival on the scene, like *Leave*

It to Beaver, Ozzie and Harriet, and *Father Knows Best.* The biggest problem those families faced was, "Oh, my God, the roast is ruined and the boss is coming to dinner!" Or "Holy moley! Mom dented the fender of Dad's car! How do we keep him from finding out?" How about the message those shows were sending? For two decades America was being told it had no race issues, no bigotry, no wars, no health problems, no unwanted pregnancies. How nifty! It was certainly expressing a point of view, as all art has a way of doing. But at what level? What impact?

I'm not going to compare myself to Lear on any level, but those words resonate because, for nearly fifty years, I've tried to find meaningful stories about how people live their lives. I taught a writing class for several years at Cal State Los Angeles, and on the first day of each semester, I read aloud the following quote from *Storycraft,* by Jack Hart, to my students:

> Storytelling has such wide application because, at its root, it serves universal human needs. Story makes sense out of a confusing universe by showing us how one action leads to another. It teaches us how to live by discovering how our fellow human beings overcome the challenges in their lives and it helps us discover the universals that bind us to everything around us. Ultimately the common ingredient in all great storytelling is the love of story itself.[5]

If you believe in that, as I do, you never stop learning. I received something of an education in college, but I've been in postgrad studies for nearly half a century now, learning on the job. "Journalism keeps you planted in the earth," Ray Bradbury allegedly said.

"Aren't you expected to grow, learn more about yourself, learn more about the world? You are when you're young," Lear said at ninety-three in a *New York Times* video interview. "Why would you be less expected to grow when you're eighty? The culture dictates how you behave, and maybe the elderly buy into it, the way they grow old. My role here now is to say wait a minute. That's not all there is. There's a good time to be had at this age."[6]

In my conversation with him, Lear challenges the notion that I have a binary choice to make, a choice between staying in or jumping out. He suggests it's possible I don't have the luxury of a choice at all. The more we talk about our interests and our work, he comes around to the realization that, like him, I'm engaged and curious and I know only one way to manage that affliction. I write.

"You're working every minute," he says. "Wherever you look ... you're working. ... You're sixty-seven, you're in good health, you have a strong mind, and you woke up to talk to Norman Lear. My God, how wonderful is that? You just poke about, loving what you do."

It's a pretty good deal, Mr. Lear. I know that. Just like it's pretty cool that I never know what my "next" is going to be. But I know it'll be an adventure. And yet, while I love all of that, the stress of organizing coherent thoughts is taxing, and like any writer, nothing I ever write feels good enough. And I always feel like I'm missing out on other things I might like to do with my time. I'd like to travel more, I tell Lear. Relax more. Fall into different routines than the same ones I've known for the entirety of my adult life.

Lear listens, but he isn't backing off. If I were to book six months in Barcelona, he says, how long do I think it would be before I begin thinking about a travel story I might pitch? Good question. In fact, I've thought about tracing my grandparents' roots in Europe and studying the forces that made them leave their homes. It would be a book about taking risks, leaving the known for the unknown.

"Wherever you go in the world," Lear says, "and wherever you wake up, so long as you have a pencil and a piece of paper, you're working."

Yes, I'm sure that for years to come, that will be my curse, even if it's a blessed curse.

"You can always write," he says, "and if you don't write, it may be that you are denying yourself a pleasure that has served you well in your work."

I tell Lear that Mel Brooks suggested I keep my job but cut back and enjoy the best of both worlds. Lear doesn't think that's such a bad idea, but the more he talks, the more it seems as though he is telling me not to stress over trying to figure it out. Just get into the hammock, live in the moment, enjoy the privilege, and move on.

"I want, when this conversation is over, for you to feel deeply what you said. You acknowledged that you can be traveling and writing," Lear tells me, saying the best of both worlds is within reach. "It's not retirement. It's on to the next."

FIFTEEN

I WAS GRATEFUL FOR THE INSIGHTS FROM MEL BROOKS AND Norman Lear, but I needed to talk to people who were no longer reporting for work each day. I needed to talk to some regular folks. And the nice people at Leisure World Seal Beach, just south of Los Angeles, have done me a favor. They've agreed to print a guest column, by me, in the retirement community's newspaper. In the column, I'm asking for guidance from the residents, most of whom are retired, a small percentage of whom are still working.

Leisure World is a modest gated community of small apartments and condos that sell in the $200,000 to $500,000 range. For a beach community in Southern California, that's cheap, and the waves are only a mile or two away.

"For those of you who are still working, are you hoping to retire soon?" I asked in the column. "For those of you who are retired, do you wish you had worked longer or retired earlier?"

I asked them to email me their thoughts and their phone numbers, so we'll see how it goes. But I'm pretty sure this will be a good way for me to go to school on the experiences of people from a wide spectrum of careers. I've been to Leisure World before, and I know the residents include former teachers, law enforcement officers, insurance agents, marketing reps, and just about every other profession.

It's early February, and if I stick to my plan, I've got five months to decide whether to retire. I find myself still wavering and influenced most by the last person I've spoken to. Norman Lear was perhaps the deepest thinker of them all, and I've given a lot of thought to his notion of living in the moment, not that my personality is suited to such an approach. I like to plan ahead. I want to begin imagining and planning my next vacation and even my next meal. I do appreciate Lear's idea of there always being a next, but in the current moment I don't know what my next might be. And what's more important, I'm not sure I know what I want it to be.

What I do know is that during the last year I've gradually adapted to life without an office to escape to. Alison is getting fairly steady work as a freelance writer, and I'm home most days except for some occasional travel to interview subjects for my column. But the tension of being under the same roof for days on end has dissipated to where I no longer feel like we'd constantly be on each other's nerves if I retire. Alison is a far more social being than I, and she's been meeting friends regularly for hikes or backyard chats. That might be her way of making sure to not have to put up with too much of me or of training herself to survive the extra closeness my retirement would bring. I, too, am beginning to spend more time with friends. Three pals and I just got together for beer and a game of backyard cornhole and I'm meeting up with my tennis buddies for an occasional game or cigar. It could be that Alison and I, consciously or subconsciously, are beginning to prepare for the fall, when we'll have the biggest "over and next" of our lives to deal with.

—℁—

For me, the college process was nothing like it is today. My parents, who worked in the mom-and-pop grocery stores of their immigrant parents, didn't go to college. It wasn't even a consideration for them. In 1971, when I graduated from the same high school my parents attended in the small San Francisco Bay Area town of Pittsburg, I knew I'd be going to college. I was convinced, as were many in my generation, that a college education put you in line for a better job, whatever it might be. With decent grades, but nothing spectacular, and no way to pay for an elite college even if I managed to be accepted by one, my path was clear. Go to a junior college for two years, then move on to a four-year state college in California, and then go find a job. That's exactly what I did, finishing up at San Jose State University on a Tuesday night, and using my journalism degree to start work the very next morning at a small newspaper in Davis, California. With my fancy BA and all my college smarts, my job as a sportswriter was to cover a combination of Little League baseball and adult recreation league softball. It wasn't much, but it was a start. If I could turn back the clock, though, I wouldn't have gone to college after high school. Not immediately, anyway. I would have traveled, taken risks, learned new ways, gotten lost. Of course, I say that now with the wisdom of experience and with regrets for having immediately gotten on the career track before checking out a world I knew nothing about. All of which may be one reason retirement appeals to me so much now. It's a chance to live the life on which I took a pass.

Fifty years later, college in the United States is a racket. I paid just a few hundred dollars a year for my degree, which is probably several thousand dollars in today's money. But lots of families today will do anything for the chance to send their kids to $75,000-a-year universities. They'll even cheat. We've just come through one of the most odious scandals in college history, with wealthy parents—some of them celebrities— paying bribes to secure placement for their children. In Los Angeles, prosecutors said actress Lori Loughlin and her fashion designer husband, Mossimo Giannulli, paid $500,000 to get their daughters into the University of Southern California as fake recruits to the school's crew team. And the girls didn't even have any rowing experience. One of the daughters said on social media that she didn't even want to go to USC, but she looked forward to attending the parties. USC, by the way, is in a neighborhood where, each year, a small number of low-income high school students, against all odds, do well enough to be accepted to elite schools but can't attend them. Even with scholarships, their families can't afford the incidental costs, housing and travel expenses, so the students opt instead for low-priced public schools closer to home, sometimes because they're expected to continue taking care of older or younger family members or get jobs and contribute to household expenses. It's a reality that made me wish all the cheaters, whether they went to prison or not, would have been forced by the courts to pay into scholarship funds for low-income students.

I'm unabashedly fond of Caroline, but we haven't set aside a college admission bribery fund for her, so she's going to have to make it on her own. She's a kid who knows what she wants, and she's made some good choices already. Though she loves competitive tennis and had the potential to become a Division I college player if she made the sport a singular focus, she couldn't bring herself to give up her other interests. So she signed up for the glee club and the Outdoors Club, worked on the school newspaper, started a satirical underground newspaper with friends, attended weekend art classes that began when she was in grade school, and played varsity sports other than tennis, including basketball, softball, soccer, and volleyball. Her goal is to enjoy a similarly well-rounded experience in college, and playing tennis at the Division III level will make that possible.

Still, I wish the process of finding and getting into the right school weren't so relentlessly pressurized as it is for her and her peers. A seventeen-year-old who's muddling through a stay-at-home pandemic has enough on her mind without the suffocating competition around college counseling, test preparation, résumé padding, peer pressure, and all the rest. Caroline has not been on campus her entire senior year of high school. Classes are Zoomed, as are friendships, at least to a degree. Instead of a victory lap, her senior year has become a drag, and it's looking ever more likely that, because of travel limitations, Caroline will have to make a decision without the advantage of checking out the campuses on her list.

"I can't believe this is what it's come to," says Alison, who loses sleep over what's been lost, as well as the uncertainty that lies ahead. We both wonder who's got it worse, the students who missed the chance to enjoy senior year on campus, or the students who spent their first year of college staring into computers in their own homes. "They've both gotten screwed," she says, and I can't disagree with that. But we do keep reminding ourselves that, all things considered, we're still healthy and damn lucky, given the hardship and loss around the country and the world. I'm telling myself to be as low key about college as possible, so Caroline doesn't feel any additional pressure. But we're all a little tense. In her pocket is a ticket to Bard, the first school she got into, but it doesn't have the greatest tennis program, and her goal is to combine a good school with a good tennis program. She hasn't yet figured out a career path, but she's interested in literature and earth sciences and thinks she may want to be a teacher.

And what will I become? A proud but blubbering dad. As time grows short, I think about it more and more. I think about it in the macro sense, as in, she'll be away for months at a time and may never again permanently live with us. And I think about it in the micro sense, as in, when we go to the supermarket we won't be buying the things Caroline likes to eat. Trader Joe's is going to be selling far less frozen mac and cheese. It won't be as much fun for me to make risotto cakes with fontina cheese and arugula salad, which she loves, or cabernet braised short ribs with mashed potatoes and roasted carrots. I've begun walking into her bedroom when she's not home and imagining it as empty space. I'll miss her classmate and pandemic buddy Quintynn, who pops into the house and chats with me and Alison and then disappears into Caroline's bedroom, and Alison and I smile at each other when we hear them giggling or cackling over something goofy, like a TikTok video they're putting together—something that often involves jumping on the bed, falling on the floor, and banging on the walls. I have no idea what the hell is going on in there. I will miss her coming home from tennis practice so pumped up and fitness minded that she immediately begins preparing a health food concoction of grains and vegetables, only to then run out for a pint of ice cream or a bag of Sour Patch Kids. I will miss watching *Jeopardy!* with Caroline and Alison, Alison keeping score as we play at home, with the two of them in competition for first place, while I lumber in, always back of the pack. High school has been gruesomely demanding for Caroline, but she's gotten a really good education and she is more than ready for college.

―⁓―

It's February 9, a chilly, gray morning. I shower and go into the closet for something I have not worn in a year: a pair of slacks, a sports coat, a necktie. The sports coat fits much better than it did the last time. I am down to 206 pounds, having lost fourteen pounds in five weeks, motivated in part by the sudden death of Tom LaBonge. Alison and I are on our way to his funeral.

There could not be a better final resting place for Tom than Forest Lawn, which sits on the north-facing slopes of the Hollywood Hills. He had told his wife, Brigid, that if he were to die, this was where he wanted to be buried. Not because he would be near the graves of Bette Davis, Lucille Ball, Gene Autry, Buster Keaton, Stan Laurel, Liberace, Debbie Reynolds, and Carrie Fisher, among other celebrities in the ground here. But because he would be adjacent to his beloved Griffith Park.

Ten days earlier, Mayor Garcetti had announced that the Mount Hollywood Summit—where LaBonge threw me the touchdown pass the day we hiked there together—would now be known as the Tom LaBonge Summit. You can't see it from the cemetery, but just over the ridge is the famous Hollywood sign, and I'm reminded of one particular outing I had with Tom. Back when the human race evolved to the point where just about everyone had a GPS app on their phone, all the secrets of access to the Hollywood sign were exposed to the entire world. Instead of having to know Los Angeles and how to negotiate the narrow, winding streets and trails that snake through its hills, everyone now had easy access to the best places to take in the Hollywood sign. This meant that once-quiet neighborhoods had become stuffed with nonstop traffic, and many of them wanted Councilman LaBonge to do something about it. He came up with several ideas, but his grandest—which never materialized—was to build a tram that would take people up to the Hollywood sign from roughly the very ground in which he was about to be laid to rest.

Alison and I park the car and begin walking up the hill to Tom's gravesite. We bump into friends and I spot various public officials who are here to pay their respects. A look of disbelief lingers in everyone's eyes. It's still too soon to accept that a man so full of life is gone. I bump into someone with the city recreation and parks department who appears stricken. She says that Tom, termed out for five years, had still been dropping by one of the parks department offices on a near-daily basis, just to check in with friends and former colleagues and see what was going on.

I want to be alone with my thoughts, so I move off to one side of the gathering as people assemble in front of the microphone. City helicopters are making a pass over the burial site, a final salute to a fallen champion. I look up at the lone tree that stands on Cahuenga Peak at an elevation of just above eighteen hundred feet. Tom and I had talked about the tree and the poems, blessings, and other thoughts hikers write, placing their notes in a bag that hangs from one of the branches. The view from that peak is spectacular. You stand on the shoulder of the mountain and feel like a bird, a hang glider, a floater. You can see the vastness of the San Fernando Valley, the Los Angeles basin, and the clear blue Pacific, with Catalina Island off in the distance. I once found a note at the tree written by someone named Susan. "This is my church," she wrote. "I feel like I'm receiving a special blessing each time I come."

Father Greg Boyle, also a friend of Tom's, is the first speaker. They were two of a kind in one regard. The priest, born seven months after me, had told me on my recent visit that his work gives him a sense of purpose and a chance to serve others. And the councilman, born nine days before me, might still be working if the city charter didn't require him to step down after serving three terms in elected office. Father Greg, who has traveled the nation and the world to talk about the young men he has spent his life serving, tells the assembled mourners a story about bumping into LaBonge in a hotel in Berlin, the city Tom had told me we should visit together. In his eulogy, Father Greg describes himself as somewhat shy and reserved and Tom as the exact opposite. He says he watched Tom greet everyone he met at that hotel, asking if they'd been to Los Angeles, asking if they'd like to come, and asking them something about themselves.

"People say if you think there's good in everybody, you haven't met everybody. Tom nearly met everybody and found good there," Father Greg says. "This is what made him the shape of God's heart. He would pull the favor out of you… and when he left your presence… you felt favorable. And you felt inclined to do this with other people so that they, too, could inhabit their unshakable goodness.

"He was like the Zen saying, 'the finger pointing to the moon is not the moon.' Tom knew he wasn't the moon, but it was his singular joy to point beyond himself to the God who loves us without measure and without regret."

Around me, people are nodding. They're wiping their eyes.

Father Greg says Tom had visited him just a few days before Christmas, in the same tent at which the padre had greeted me.

As Tom left him that day, Father Greg says, he had these parting words for the padre: "There's good in everybody. Ya just have to wait for it."

"Tom left," says Father Greg, "and I felt favorable. The shape of God's heart."

SIXTEEN

THE RESIDENTS OF LEISURE WORLD SEAL BEACH HAVE WEIGHED in, and they had a lot to say. After my queries about retirement were published in the *Golden Rain News*, emails flooded my in-basket, and the downpour lasted for days.

"My advice about retiring is don't even think about it," said one resident.

"I am about to retire and can't wait!" said another.

"I find myself dealing with depression and loneliness. I don't feel I have a purpose in life," said yet another.

That's how it went, a mix of contentedness, coping, disappointment, regret, and perseverance. The wide spectrum of responses wasn't particularly surprising, given differences in health, income, and social connections, all of which are factors in aging well. A 2017 study by AARP found that two-thirds of people sixty and older were either satisfied or extremely satisfied with their lives, but one-third are either not very satisfied or not at all satisfied.[1]

"For no one I know did retirement work out like they'd planned," wrote a seventy-eight-year-old Leisure World resident named John. "Travel ideas don't work out for many different reasons. Kids move away. Teen granddaughters get pregnant. Unexpected costs delete savings quickly."

I drove to Leisure World one day and went to lunch with John, who told me that as a young man, he lost a marketing job he loved, and it seemed that he still felt the sting of rejection. "When you have a boss who doesn't want you, there's nothing you can do about it," said John, who taught for a while and took on other jobs that got him to the finish line in reasonably good financial shape.

He was much more upbeat about retirement than he had been in his emails and during a phone conversation. But Leisure World did take a while to get used to, John said, and it felt kind of cliquish. His wife thought they were too young to be there, so they both took delight in seeing a resident pushing a stroller one day. "We thought, 'Oh, how nice, there are some kids here,'" John said, thinking a resident was out for a stroll with a grandchild. Then they got a closer look. The stroller passenger was a pet.

But it didn't take long for John and his wife to settle in and feel at home. Their list of activities included Spanish club, shuffleboard, and Rotary. John joined the impaired vision and hearing club, and he and his wife attended Long Beach Symphony concerts and went on a lot of cruises. At lunch, he got out his cellphone and did something I occasionally do. He looked up the ages of famous people at the time of their death. George Segal, Mother Teresa, Margaret Thatcher, Helen Keller, Gregory Peck, and Ruth Bader Ginsburg all died at eighty-seven. Why was John looking up that particular age? Average life expectancy for men is seventy-eight, said John. His age. But if you make it that far, "now your life expectancy is eighty-seven."

I knew that if Alison had taken the trip to Leisure World with me, she would have felt the same way John's wife did initially.

But I'm older than she is, and for any pensioner who wants to live in California near the beach at an affordable price, Leisure World—one of the first retirement communities in the nation—has a lot going for it. Built in the 1960s, it's not exactly luxury living, but the amenities include swimming, golf, an amphitheater, a post office, and medical facilities.

I couldn't meet face-to-face with other residents because they were still being cautious about the virus, but I spent weeks exchanging emails and phone calls with my new posse of retirement counselors. One of my favorite emails was from a woman named Jane, who took a number of hairpin turns after working for twenty-eight years as a paralegal in the patent department of a toy company.

> It was a demanding, interesting job and I hated to leave, but I was getting up there in years, and so at age 66, I decided to retire. My boss and the employees in the law department gave me a big sendoff, with a party, presents, the works. I was happy as I gathered my things from my cubicle, bid goodbye, and drove away from the big parking lot for the last time.

Reading the email, I pictured myself in Jane's shoes, driving away for the last time. How would I feel? More mixed than Jane did, I'm pretty sure. But there's more to her story.

> The following Monday morning, I got up, took a shower, got dressed, had breakfast and then, as I was sipping my second cup of coffee, I realized it was 8 a.m. and I was all dressed up with no place to go. I tried to stay busy during the week by cleaning my condo thoroughly, doing some painting (I am a Sunday painter), and other little jobs, but I had a sinking feeling that

I had made a mistake. I loved working, and now there was no place for me to go and nothing for me to do.

It sounded like a serious case of buyer's remorse. But Jane fixed her unexpected problem in a hurry.

After another week of this, I could stand it no longer, so I called my boss and asked him if I could come back. Thankfully, he said "Sure!" and so the following week, I found myself back at my desk, doing the same job. But this time my employment was handled by a temp agency. I was being paid more money for the same job, and I only had to work three days a week! It was great!

Jane says she worked another three years after going back, but the office environment changed in that time and the collegiality she had enjoyed became but a memory.

Around this time, the company began "cleaning house" and laying people off, as they did periodically, and my boss told me one morning that one of the people that they were laying off was me. Actually, I was relieved. It was time to go… for real.

I'm not likely to make the mistake of retiring without a clue as to what I want to do. But that doesn't mean I can anticipate how I'll feel in the early stages of retirement. Might I travel? Yes. Might I do some volunteer work for a cause I care about? Yes. Write more books? I hope so. Spend more time reading and taking long walks? Affirmative. But in my head, at the moment, I'm not sure I wouldn't miss what I do now and regret leaving the largest and best newspaper in the West when no one is asking me to do so.

Ellen, eighty-seven, decided in the course of reaching out to me that maybe she should be writing a memoir.

> I think I've had many lives, like a cat, and I could write a book about each one (maybe I will) . . . With each of these lives, I lost people, parents, aunts, school friends, sorority sisters, bicycle buddies, senior Olympians, church staff, children grew up, husbands died, and so on. At the same time, new acquaintances came in. We kept something and some friends from each life. Things we learned carried over. It's all in our memory. Experience all you can. It's a beautiful world.

Ellen competed in the 2011 Summer National Senior Games in Houston. In the 75–79 age group, she came in fourth in the discus throw, with a toss of 16.18 meters, and third in the javelin competition, with a throw of 15.21 meters. I wish I'd been there to cheer her on.

It might not be possible to age any more gracefully than Ellen, but a retired hospital administrator named Marty, seventy-five, is doing pretty well after a career that ended with mounting stress.

> I knew I was hitting the wall, so to speak, when I found myself not caring about the job or, more importantly, patient care. I began to plan my retirement about a year before I finally left. My wife gave up her business manager position with a hospital chain. I've always wanted to teach and found myself being an assistant professor for healthcare management for six years. Then it was on to full retirement, with a move to Leisure World. I've found time to spend hours reading, playing with grandkids, attending Synagogue, and traveling to Europe every other year and continuing my enjoyment of wine. So, I'm happy; my wife

is happy. Couple of old-age issues, but all in all it's an enjoyable last quarter of my life.

Last quarter of life? I hadn't considered my life in percentages like that, perhaps because it's so depressing to do the math. If I'm already three-quarters of the way to the finish line, it means I've got twenty-three years left, which would take me to about ninety. Maybe, as we age, we live in denial about how fast the clock is moving.

One Leisure World resident told me she had turned in her retirement papers at the public university where she teaches. She has loved teaching, she said, but she was satisfied with the contribution she had made. She wanted to chase other pursuits, including the study of Buddhism, and she wanted to hand the baton to the next generation of professors.

In the last couple of years, the *Los Angeles Times* has added three columnists, all much younger than I. My newest colleagues have interests, skills, backgrounds, and perspectives I don't have, all of which is good, because the newspaper business will surely die without cultivating younger readers. But we have another columnist who's about ten years older than I am, and he shows no signs of slowing down. George Skelton covers government and politics in our Sacramento bureau, and his knowledge, institutional memory, skill, and objectivity are all great assets to the *Los Angeles Times*. The audience for the print version of newspapers is shrinking, but those still hanging on tend to be older. I'd like to think I write about people and topics that interest them, and I hope I change things up enough to attract younger readers now and then. Everyone does, however, have to pass the baton at some point.

The Leisure World resident who wrote to say "my advice about retiring is don't even think about it" is a freelance writer, still working. Her neighbors seem to be having a swell time playing shuffleboard, Ping Pong, and golf, but none of that appeals to her.

I plan on doing this until I drop. When I think to myself sometimes that it would be nice not to have the pressures that come with this kind of work, I remind myself that it is far better than what I see my neighbors doing, and I am happy that I have purpose and work that sometimes is so engrossing that I lose track of time.

That's a line I can relate to. When I'm writing, I lose track of time. When I'm not, the clock slows, and I don't mean that in a good way. I get blasé, antsy, moody. You could ask Alison. The freelance writer went on to say:

The only people I see who seem to enjoy retirement are those who have a lot of grandkids, or who are able to travel a lot, or those who hated their jobs, or those who are passionate about other pursuits that retirement has finally given them a chance to pursue. If none of this describes you, I think retirement would become really boring for you.

Mike, another Leisure World resident, gave me a similar warning. After a number of different jobs, he became a writer for a magazine that eventually went under, and he wishes it hadn't.

One day you have responsibilities and duties and people count on you for your contributions. The next day, day one of retirement, you have nowhere to go, nothing to do, and worst of all, no one is counting on you, expecting you to provide whatever it is you have done so well for so long.

Finding hobbies and joining clubs can help, Mike said. But only to a point.

> They give you a reason to crawl out from under the covers. But unless you are the captain of the bowling team, no one will miss you if you don't show up at the hobby hour . . . Once you are a retiree you are no longer needed. If you can learn to live with that, fine. Just don't expect retirement to be very fulfilling. Cause it ain't.

Depression and feelings of isolation are surely not uncommon at this stage of life. I know that from decades of talking to people fighting the forces of time, and I recall my mother saying—as physical and cognitive limitations gradually transformed life for her and my father—that the golden years are not so golden. But that's all the more reason to admire those who find peace in the struggle, cutting bargains they can live with. One such person, a Leisure World resident named William, was a college professor whose health challenges forced him to reinvent himself when he was in his 50s.

> As my mind started to reknit, I took stock of what skills I could assemble to create a minimally acceptable version of myself. I'm still laboring on that task of reconstruction, but I've realized, so is everyone. From infancy to death, this skill improves, this skill declines, so that you wake up a slightly different person than you were the day before . . . It was a hard journey for me, and I'm still

accruing layer after sedimentary layer of refurbished me. I anticipate you have a higher profile than I ever had, so you must be certain there's a Steve Lopez who doesn't feel empty when he's not complimented, or yelled at, for today's column.

I wished I could have rounded up William and all the others who sent me their heart-felt thoughts and words of advice and thrown a big party for them at Leisure World. They took my inquiry seriously, and their responses gave me a deeper understanding of both the risks and rewards of retirement. A former teacher named Fred sent me his life story and counsel in a neat little package, written like the transcript of a conversation.

I taught Fifth Grade at Valley Christian Elementary in Bellflower/Cerritos for forty years and was soccer coach at Valley Christian High School for thirty-one years, starting in 1965. Loved my job. My wife Wilma (yes, Fred and Wilma) was an RN at a nursing home (Artesia Christian Home, a really good place). She loved her job and was really good at it. Then something weird happened. We got older. Years slipped away when we weren't looking. Our bodies gave us gentle reminders. Energy levels were a little lower on the dipsticks of our lives. We looked at our finances, decided we could retire. We felt we could sell our house and leave the neighborhood. That year, 2005, Wilma said, "You retire, I retire." We retired on the same day.

Fred and Wilma sold their house and moved to Leisure World, and their first day there was an eventful one.

Neighbor lady on 3-wheel bicycle stops, curious about who's moving in. Tells me her name is Jean, and she's biking to control her diabetes. Shows me a slip from her doctor. On her next trip around the building she stops and says, "My name is Jean. I'm biking to control my diabetes. I can show you the doctor's orders." No, that's okay, Jean. I'm Fred, nice to meet you. Moments later my visiting grandson goes to a neighbor's house and rings the doorbell because he likes doorbells. So I go over to apologize to the short elderly woman who answered the door. She looks at me and says, "Welcome to the neighborhood. Say . . . you look a lot like my fourth husband." I sucker right into it. "How many husbands have you had?" "Three."

Sixteen years later, Fred is seventy-nine, Wilma seventy-three. Both are busy and happy, but Fred is not in the business of advising aspiring retirees on when the time is right.

I can only tell you that I can't tell you. Only you can. Are you determined to make it work? Will you be positive about it? Celebrate the advantages? Or . . . will your focus be on the restrictive nature of growing old in a retirement environment? Will you complain about minor inconveniences? Grouch about the behavior of certain senior citizens? If you have a positive attitude, you will find lots of company. If you have a negative attitude, you will find like-minded folks as well. You will find what you look for. There is one inevitability over which we have no control—our health. Perhaps there will be some pain and disability. We are going to die. Many of my neighbors and friends have left LW horizontally. Until then, let's make the best of it. Let gratitude be our travel companion. Gratitude for family, friends, for physical and emotional well-being, for our sense of curiosity and creativity. That gratitude is a choice. Your choice.

Thanks, Fred, and you're right. It's my choice. I don't have it all worked out yet, but I find myself inching closer to a decision.

SEVENTEEN

IN LATE FEBRUARY AND EARLY MARCH, CAROLINE HEARS from two more schools near the top of her list. She's accepted at Whitman College in Washington and Denison University in Ohio. She likes the academic offerings at both schools, and she's been in touch with the tennis coaches. I begin checking air travel connections, thinking that if it's Whitman, this could be a pretty good deal for Caroline's parents, not that we're the first consideration. But we love the Pacific Northwest, and you can get to Walla Walla by flying first to Portland or Seattle. I'm thinking seafood and salmon and Willamette Valley Pinot Noir and excursions to Florence, Tillamook, and Bandon on the Oregon coast. I'm also thinking of riding those big white-and-green ferries out of Seattle to places like Whidbey, Bainbridge, Orcas, and Lopez Island. It's not that I intend to relocate to the vicinity of Caroline's college town, it's just that I could soon be retired, so I've got to start thinking about how I want to spend my leisure time in conjunction with trips to watch her play tennis.

If it's Denison, that has plenty of advantages too. I like that it sits roughly in the middle of Cleveland, Pittsburgh, Detroit,

Louisville, Indianapolis, and Cincinnati, most of which I've visited but don't know particularly well. Alison is most excited about Denison, not just because it's highly regarded and not just because it's the closest school to where her mother lives. She grew up in Pennsylvania and went to the University of North Carolina, and she puts a high value on the experience of going to school in a state other than the one you grew up in. It's new. It's different. It's challenging. And being a long way from home is an education in itself.

Okay, sure. But come on. This is my baby girl. I don't disagree with any of Alison's arguments for Denison or any of the other schools that seem a million miles from our home, but Caroline's fast-approaching departure is going to be hard enough to handle. The farther she goes, the emptier our nest is going to feel for me. Maybe it's something about the relationships between fathers and daughters. Maybe it's something about my stage in life and the fact that, when my sons went off to college, I still had most of my career ahead of me. But I'm now a full-fledged senior citizen, and the thought of all three of my kids being in the eastern time zone still strikes me as more than a little depressing. I'm being selfish, I know, and this isn't about me, it's about Caroline. I'm just being honest about the fact that I'm going to miss the hell out of her.

"She's going to be fine wherever she goes," says Alison, who is the voice of reason at the moment, if not always. I, too, know she'll be okay. I think playing competitive tennis for twelve years is one reason for Caroline's ability to handle pressure and uncertainty. It's an individual sport and you're out there by yourself. You learn how to win and you learn how to lose. That's the nature of the game; it's the way of life.

Heading into the third week of March, what seems like the longest year in history—thanks to the pandemic, thanks to Caroline's high school campus being locked down, and thanks to a solid year of playing the college navigation game—is now coming to a close. Caroline has applied to ten schools in all. She has been accepted at eight of them. And she thinks she knows where she's headed. Denison's tennis team is ranked higher nationally in Division III than any of the other schools on her list. It has the earth science and literature curriculum she's after. It's the next state over from Caroline's grandmother, her aunt and uncle, her cousins. She texts the coach, just to check in and let her know that Denison is still one of her top choices. The coach calls her, and after they chat for a while, Caroline hands me the phone. I'm a little surprised, because Caroline is so determined to do things on her own, and I don't want to interfere with that. But I grab the phone and say hello to coach Jamie Scott and tell her we're all excited about the possibility of Caroline attending Denison. Then I ask how her roster looks in the coming year. The coach tells me she's losing four players to graduation and she's recruiting four freshmen, including Caroline. If we feel it's safe to do so, Scott says, we should consider traveling to Ohio this weekend for Denison's first match of the season, a home affair against Ohio Wesleyan.

As noted, there's some risk in choosing a four-year college without ever having visited the campus, so we book the trip. We fly from Burbank to Phoenix for a brief layover and then on to Columbus, a nice midsize city I've enjoyed visiting in the past. We get a rental car and I drive over to a neighborhood called the Short North Arts District, which isn't far from the Ohio State University campus. Denison is in the tiny town of Granville, and I figure Caroline will be more comfortable when she discovers that Columbus is a real city and it's only half an hour away. We drive up and down High Street in the Short North, taking in several blocks of commercial buzz, with coffee joints, restaurants, quirky shops, and lots of young people on the streets. Alison likes what she sees. Caroline likes what she sees. And then we're on to Granville.

The weather gods have cooperated. We could have been in for a late freeze at this time of year, but the sun is shining, the temperature is in the sixties, the spring bloom has begun. There isn't much to downtown Granville, just a few square blocks in the tiny burg of about five thousand residents. But what's here—neat rows of two-story brick structures built in the nineteenth and twentieth centuries—was designed for a postcard. Students wearing red Denison gear stroll along East Broadway. There's a line outside Whit's Frozen Custard, and at Broadway and Main Street is St. Luke's, a Greek Revival Episcopal Church built in 1837. Early settlers came from Granville, Massachusetts, which is how the place got its name, and it's often described as resembling a New England village.

"This is so sweet," Alison exclaims.

Caroline has her eye on something else. She's studied photos and the layout of the campus that sits on the wooded hill that rises over the town.

"That's Swasey Chapel," she says, pointing out the red-brick-and-limestone structure that stands in the center of the 250-acre campus.

We spend half an hour driving through the campus. Thanks to the spring weather, students are out in shorts and flip-flops. Some of them are lounging in big red Adirondack chairs splayed on the grass near the student union. We drive down to the far side of the campus, past the football stadium, and over to the athletic center, with twelve outdoor tennis courts and four more indoor courts. Caroline likes what she sees. We all do.

We check into a hotel and return the next day just in time for the Denison–Ohio Wesleyan match. Again, the weather is perfect, and the Denison men's tennis team has gathered to cheer on the women's team. We meet the athletic director, Coach Scott, and most of the team members, many of whom trot over to introduce themselves to Caroline. The university president, Adam Weinberg, is also watching the match, and he welcomes us to the campus. Weinberg, formerly a dean at Colgate University, tells us that on his first visit to Denison, he called his wife and told her, "There's something magical about this place." Weinberg asks Caroline what she wants to study and tells her about some upcoming additions to the earth studies program. At this point, I'm feeling so comfortable here, I'm ready to enroll. I'd have to make sure they didn't see my high school transcripts, though. Or my college transcripts, for that matter. But it all feels so welcoming, and we're reminded that while some of the schools Caroline applied to responded with form letters, Denison was a little different. Caroline received a handwritten note from an admissions officer who commented on her application essay, and she was offered an academic scholarship that brings tuition pretty close to what we would have paid if she had attended school at one of California's UCs. And here she is now talking to the university president, who is telling us that, among other Denison selling points, most of the bitter winter weather in Ohio hits a wall about forty miles north of campus, sparing Granville. I don't know if a word of it is true, but I know that we're all feeling pretty good about things at this point.

There is no school mascot, which some might consider a deficiency. No badgers, gophers, hedgehogs, cougars, or bears. But everyone keeps saying "Let's go, Big Red," which stands as both the school color and de facto athletic nickname.

And the Big Red women take every match, beating Ohio Wesleyan, 9–0, with victories in singles and doubles by Alex Cash, Sydney and Hannah Cianciola, Sarah Robertson, Kendall Schrader, Monique Brual, Hannah Bradvica, and Devin Gramley, most of whom will be Caroline's teammates if she chooses this school.

That night, back at the hotel, Caroline gets out her computer. She turns it on, navigates to the Denison website, and commits.

I know she could not have made a better choice.

And I know that when we bring her back here in August, wish her the best, and wave goodbye, we're going to have a long ride home.

EIGHTEEN

FOR MANY YEARS I SKIPPED ANNUAL PHYSICAL EXAMS. I figured I was in pretty good health, so why endure the prodding, probing, and general inconvenience of a checkup? That's a bad policy, for obvious reasons, a point driven home by my brief experience as a human cadaver in the summer of 2012. I was fifty-eight at the time, an age at which you begin to hear the disheartening news that contemporaries are struggling with various health problems. I've been a little more vigilant since my lights blinkered out, and over the last several months of interviews with retirees, I've heard over and over again how illness can ruin your best-laid plans. So I'm now down for annual checkups, no dumb excuses accepted.

At the last visit, my doctor asked how I was doing.

"Pretty good," I said. As you get older, you realize nobody really wants to hear about all your nagging little signs of accelerated demise. But a doctor has no choice in the matter, so I rattled off a list of ailments, from clogged sinuses to blurry eyes to various aches and pains that might be associated with having knees full of nuts and bolts.

"Well, you're lucky," my doctor said with not one ounce of sympathy.

"How so?" I asked.

"Because you've lived long enough to experience all of that," he said.

That's one way to look at it. Maybe I really am lucky in the sense that I don't have any major medical issues at the moment. But when I turn on the television, I figure it won't be long before something goes wrong. Judging by the barrage of pharmaceutical ads, many of them aimed at pensioners, I'm past due for regular trials with constipation, hearing loss, and toe fungus, among other maladies.

Some of the people in these commercials look like nice enough folks, and I guess it's a good thing that they're making a few bucks hawking prescription drugs. But that doesn't mean I don't harbor ill will toward them after the fiftieth or sixtieth time they pop up on my screen. A hard hat named Frank decides, at a construction site, to tell us about opioid-induced constipation and the miracle of Movantik. "I tried prunes, laxatives, still constipated. I talked to my doctor, and she said, how long have you been holding this in?" Frank laughs at his own joke, which doesn't get any funnier in daily repeat performances. After his quip, Frank says, "That was my Movantik moment."

I'm thrilled that Frank found relief, but the cynic in me wonders about the ethics of using actors to peddle drugs to strangers, cutting out the middleman, who in this case is a physician. It's not like they're selling pillows or refrigerators. They're selling medical advice, and even if you have to get a prescription from your doctor, isn't it a little strange that you've self-diagnosed on the basis of a television ad, and now you're advising the physician on what kind of medicine you need?

"Jardiance can help save your life from a heart attack or stroke," says the voice-over on an ad for the diabetes 1 medication.

Can it?

The lady in one Jardiance ad gets a break, in my book, because she wasn't given great material to work with. She's forced to strut in place before leading a high school marching band onto a football field, and the music sticks in your head for hours after you hear it, but not in a good way.

"Here's your favorite commercial again," Alison says whenever it comes on, because she delights it knowing how irritating I find this thing.

While the woman in the ad is performing, we hear a voice begin to rattle off the various side effects that can occur with Jardiance, and there's so much there, you keep waiting for them to add that your eyeballs may pop out of your head like birdshot and injure nearby loved ones. In this particular ad we're informed that you might come down with a case of keto-acidosis, "a serious side effect that may be fatal." Also, "a rare but life-threatening infection in the skin of the perineum could occur." Okay, what is the perineum and where is it? There's a word crawl in the commercial, but the text is tiny and it's rolling by in a flash, so I went to the Jardiance website for more information and spent about half a day reading about all the potential side effects. One of them is called "necrotizing fasciitis," which is "a rare but serious bacterial infection that causes damage to the tissue under the skin in the area between and around your anus and genitals." So now we've located the perineum. I'm familiar with that area, and I'm sure I don't want any of the noted side effects going on down there. You're also looking at the possibility of "yeast infection of the penis," which could lead to "foul-smelling discharge from the penis," none of which makes it into the television ad.[1]

Look, if I'm taking on all those risks from a pill, I want to be able to do a lot more than high step onto the high school football field wearing white gloves and a blazer. I want to play quarterback for the Green Bay Packers or get shot into space, something worth all the trouble of pushing back against the aging process.

If you happen to be the nervous type, or you're inclined in the least toward hypochondria, you're better off not turning on the television at all after the age of sixty, because you're nothing but a sitting duck, and Big Pharma is gunning for you day and night. You'd think we're adrift in a sea of disease, and the moment we fear losing our homes because of medical expenses, Tom Selleck pops up to shill for reverse mortgage companies that would be happy to work out an arrangement for us.

But when it comes to TV, we old-timers just can't wean ourselves, can we? The country is aging faster than ever before in history, and the older we get, the more we watch television. In its latest accounting, the Bureau of Labor Statistics reported that people in the sixty-five-to-seventy-four age group spend about twenty minutes a day exercising, about twenty-five minutes socializing, forty-five minutes reading, and four and a half hours watching television.[2] You don't need a medical degree to know those are unhealthy numbers. In the seventy-five-and-up group, the daily averages are less than fifteen minutes of exercise, less than thirty minutes socializing, almost an hour reading, and more than five hours watching television. Other surveys put the amount of daily television watching at six or seven hours for those sixty-five and older, but whether it's four, five, six, or seven hours, we're a captive audience, and a gullible one too.

A team of researchers from Yale University concluded that direct-to-consumer (DTC) ads, as these are called, raise all sorts of issues. "We found that DTC ads frequently contained information that could be considered misleading," said the study, which also concluded that "the overall quality of information provided in ads was low."[3] A major issue, according to the research, is that drugs are often pitched as helpful for indications not approved by the FDA. Ads for diabetes medications, for instance, often suggest they can lead to weight loss or control high blood pressure.

Of course, it's not about patient needs with these drugs. It's about convincing people they should run out and buy name-brand products—rather than less expensive generics—with ridiculous names dreamed up by marketers who laugh all the way to the bank. "Research has shown that DTC advertising for prescription drugs increases patient demand.... In 2015, spending on DTC ads in the U.S. reached $5.6 billion," the study found.[4]

If you're sitting on the couch seven hours a day watching television and exercising less than twenty minutes a day, aren't erectile dysfunction, full body fungus, and generally deteriorating health conditions guaranteed? Of course they are. But we're conditioned to think there's got to be an easy fix in pill form. It might be Trulicity, Viagra, Eliquis, Ozempic, Entyvio, or some other crazy name that sounds like a word scramble. Imagine the point totals you could rack up if only you could use prescription brand names in Scrabble.

I may not be entirely sure whether to retire or how to spend my leisure time if I do, but I'm becoming more clear on what I don't want to do. I don't want to spend hours every day subjecting myself to a marketing blitz, hoisting myself off the davenport only to answer the doorbell and collect another delivery of pharmaceuticals. Another big push in TV marketing is the prefab meal. Have you stopped to consider the genius behind that racket? I know a lot of people have busy schedules, and finding the time to shop and prepare meals can be a challenge. But come on. It's not beef Wellington or moules marinière that's coming out of those boxes. It looks like some of those dinner sacks have nothing more than a scrap of chicken with a slice of carrot and a wedge of onion. Anyone with a spatula and a pulse can throw that together in just a few minutes. And yet in the ads, dumb-struck families gather around the kitchen table as if Julia Childs has risen from the dead and sent over a care package.

If I sound like a snob, it's because I like to cook. I even like to shop. And when I do retire, I intend to spend more time ex-perimenting in the kitchen. I also intend to eat healthier food, though not always, and exercise more than twenty minutes a day, except when everything hurts at the same time.

By the way, on March 9, sixty-four days into my New Year's resolution, I went for an extra-long morning walk with Domi-nic the guard dog, then did forty-five minutes on the stationary bike. Then I stepped onto the scale, held my breath, and looked down at my feet.

The number that came up was 200.2 pounds, for a weight loss of twenty pounds in sixty-four days.

On April 2, I hit 197.4.

I'm not going to say it's been easy giving up snacks and sweets, and it pained me to have to cut back on Manhattans, old-fashioneds, ice-cold pilsners, and wine of every color. Clearing sixty to ninety minutes a day for exercise is a chal-lenge, too, for which there's a price to pay, if I have to be com-pletely honest about it.

My feet hurt. My knees hurt. And I feel like I may need a hip replacement or two sooner rather than later.

But they have drugs for those things. I've seen them on television.

NINETEEN

WHEN I WAS A KID, WE HAD A DOUGHBOY POOL IN OUR backyard, and we spent hours splashing around in it every summer. At one end of the pool was a wooden deck my dad and I built together, from which you could climb onto the roof of the house. Once in a while, when my parents weren't home, I'd go up there and stand at the edge of the roof and stare down at the water, trying to get up the nerve to jump. If I didn't break a leg or possibly my neck, it would be a heck of a thrill. Should I leap?

I feel the same way about retirement. Could be great. Could be a disaster. Or it might be anything in between. So I wanted to make sure to check in with lots of people who parachuted safely and happily into retirement, more or less.

As a rule of thumb, here's a good clue that someone's retirement is going well: when you dial their number, they answer on a boat offshore of Southern California.

"We're on a three-week cruise down to San Diego," Joan tells me when she picks up the phone, and I can hear some background chatter on her boat's marine radio. Joan says she and her husband, Ted, had made a stop in Oceanside the prior evening, and a crew of commercial fishermen offered them some of their fresh catch. So seafood is on the menu for dinner tonight, Joan says, but first there will be happy hour.

Joan lives in Leisure World Seal Beach, and she was one of the dozens who got in touch with me after I solicited advice. She worked in marketing and Ted was a general contractor. They did well enough financially to begin planning for retirement at relatively young ages, and they made the leap when Joan was fifty-three and Ted was fifty-eight. They'd done a lot of homework by then, counting up assets and liabilities, and factoring in the math on Medicare and Social Security benefits.

"We retired in 2004 and spent the next thirteen years traveling on our boat through thirty countries, twenty-eight states, and three Canadian provinces," says Joan. "Having a dream is important."

There's no way I could have retired at that age, financially speaking, nor did I have any desire to stop working. Joan says she and her husband have had no regrets seventeen years after putting their work years behind them. For those who are financially able to make the break, her advice is this: "I would say don't wait. Do it now. Do it while you're young."

I don't think I can be called young, but I'm the youngest I'll ever be from here on out. And that's what keeps me up, wondering if I'm a fool to do anything other than buy a boat and get lost at sea for weeks on end, reeling in dinner every night, and celebrating sunset with a cocktail in hand. But then I think of Mel Brooks's prediction that I'd maybe last a total of two weeks before the urge to work and write would hit once again.

Lillian, seventy, is another retirement success story. She retired two years ago after a long career as a mortgage loan officer and has no regrets. But when she reached out to me from Leisure World, she had a critical piece of advice.

"I do believe that you definitely have to be 100 percent ready to go. I was, and I've never looked back."

Lillian said she did a lot of volunteering even when she was working, but she's stepped it up in retirement and is enjoying it more. "I am a docent with the Philharmonic Society of Orange County and having so much fun attending concerts," Lillian said. She also gives tours to children at the two-hundred-year-old Mission San Juan Capistrano and volunteers as a financial planning advisor to senior citizens. And in her free time? Lillian has that covered too. "I have hiked my entire life, but there was a span of time when I hadn't been able to enjoy this activity . . . or didn't have a group to enjoy it with. Now I have joined a group of lady hikers and I am so grateful. It brings me much joy and happiness to be out with a group of fun ladies who love nature and are just as lovely themselves."

There's one more thing that keeps Lillian busy. She has a seventy-four-year-old boyfriend. He's a real estate appraiser who loves his job and will never retire, Lillian said, "but he's doing a better job of slowing it down and trying to enjoy his hobbies [cars, motorcycles, and skiing, to name a few]."

Joan and Lillian have a lot in common. They had the financial means to retire comfortably, and they knew what they wanted to do with their time. They also had someone to share the experience with.

"Retirement, I believe, should be the best time of our lives," said Lillian, and she seems to be living that dream. But the line of hers that made a bigger impression on me was the one I just mentioned: "You definitely have to be 100 percent ready to go."

Last July 4, I wasn't 100 percent ready to go. By January, in this year of anniversaries and milestones and the death of a friend, I was leaning hard toward retirement, but it wasn't a 100 percent kind of feeling. If I have a toe over the line at the moment, it's on the side of continuing to work full-time for a while longer or coming up with a hybrid plan: less work, more leisure. I wonder, though, if Lillian is right in suggesting that if you want to completely break free of work, you can't harbor a doubt or go halfway, not in your head and not in your heart. Some people, I'm sure, have the luxury of intellectual certainty. But I still think of retirement as an experiment, a time to make new discoveries rather than follow a script. Joan and Lillian planned ahead and visualized a life and identity for themselves as retirees, and the peace and well-being they describe tempts me to jump in with them. But I don't yet have a specific plan for what comes next, and what's occurred to me lately is that there might just be a possibility that I don't want one. What has kept me awake through half a century of work is surprise, variety, adventure—an organic evolution of interests and pur-suits. The job offers structure, but without boundaries. If I still don't have a good idea what the structure of my life might be in retirement, after nine months of peering through the looking glass, does that mean I'm not ready?

One day I received an unsolicited email from a reader named Peter, who wrote to say that, as a recent retiree, he has time to reach out to people who have made a difference in his life. He said he was working his way down the list and came to me, so he wanted to say that, over the years, he had sometimes agreed with me, sometimes disagreed, but he often saw things a little differently after reading one of my columns. "Sometimes, you fray my nerves," he said. "But this is not a bad thing."

I wrote back to tell Peter how flattered I was by his note, and I have truly never stopped being grateful for the privilege of connecting with readers, giving them something to think about, and getting just as much in return. But I also wanted to hear more about Peter's retirement. He wrote back and we later talked about the shape of life after a long career, which, in his case, included time as a teacher, a patrolman, a detective, an assistant sheriff, and a commissioner on the Board of Parole Hearings.

"I find myself busy managing my brother, being husband to my wife, Maria, who is a middle school counselor, traveling, and hiking and so forth, which probably sounds more recreational than career-like, but… I am unable to use the 'R word,'" Peter said. "I dislike it when friends or associates ask how I like being 'retired.' It feels diminished." Peter said he prefers to tell people that he works for himself or that he's unemployed, both of which are true.

"Maria and I don't have kids. Even though there are nieces and nephews and certainly piles of students and former students, I think that, when you don't reproduce, the passage of time (and life stages) is less linear and apparent than they would be if you did have kids, grandkids, and so forth. Transitions seem like more of a jolting slam."

I hadn't really thought of it that way, but Peter may be right. I had my first son, Jeffrey, when I was twenty-four, then along came Andrew two years later, with Caroline dropping in a quarter of a century after Jeff. So, for almost fifty years, the contours of time have been shaped by parenting and work. But when Caroline leaves, there will be more empty space in my universe, and the big transitions flying at me like meteors may strike with greater force.

I think I've conditioned myself to idealize retirement and to see it in simplistic terms, as a passage from one world to another, with a clear line of demarcation between the two. Peter described a more expansive experience, in which he has neither let go of the past nor decided on a future. He thinks about becoming a flight attendant, because he loves to travel, or a nurse, because he's always been drawn to medicine, or a paralegal or lawyer, because in law enforcement he often enjoyed the company of those in the legal profession and admired their work. Leaving his job left a void, he tells me, and though he has no regrets, because he knew it was time to go, he's still swinging in Norman Lear's hammock, suspended between what's over and what's next. He retired two years ago, Peter said, "not because I was tired of the job. I knew full well that it was gainful, meaningful, and challenging, and I miss it every single day. I miss being part of something bigger than myself. I miss the interaction with attorneys. I miss being in a position to have to produce, and produce at a high standard, under difficult conditions."

But he felt increasingly out of step with the direction of a parole board that, in his view, was releasing too many inmates who had been convicted of serious crimes. And he could hear the ticking clock. "Time in this life is limited," Peter said, "and spending it in concrete boxes with unhappy people is not ultimately a good choice."

So how does he spend his time now?

Peter rises at 4:00 a.m. in his Southern California beach town, has a cup of coffee, muses about how to spend the rest of his life, then goes for a two-and-a-half-mile run at four thirty, a chance to "view the morning sky" as if it's his alone. Then he draws up a daily list of things to do and gets started on them.

When he told me that, I couldn't let it sit. My brain is wired to ask the next question.

What's on today's list?

Peter was happy to oblige.

- Lengthy email exchange with wife's cousin in Sicily.
- Pull the trigger on buying plane tickets for a trip to Naples, with a return through Palermo.
- Take care of paperwork involving donations and scheduling for two nonprofits he works with. One is a residential facility for people with schizophrenia, which Peter's brother has dealt with for years. The other is the Nature Conservancy.
- Reconnect with a friend in Santa Barbara regarding an upcoming trip to Santa Cruz Island.
- Take used ink cartridges to Staples for recycling.
- Wash and wax his 2002 Honda Civic.
- Talk to his attorney about a special-needs trust involving his brother.
- Make dinner for himself and his wife.

Okay, that sounds like a pretty busy day, and no wonder he doesn't think of himself as retired. But once again, another question popped into my head.

What's for dinner?

"Last night was gluten-free pasta with fennel and sardines," Peter said. "Tonight is avocado halves with chicken salad, avocado mayo, and various seasonings, with some diced mango on the side and some fake chocolate pudding I've devised using nonfat yogurt with unsweetened cocoa powder and some maple syrup."

Whenever I retire, I hope to be as busy, productive, and reflective as Peter. He's sorted through the complexities of this passage and says, two years into this phase of his life, retirement has gotten neither easier nor harder. He helped illuminate for me the idea that it's okay and normal to mourn the loss of what once was while trying to figure out what might be on the horizon.

So, to answer my question, Peter said, "I still don't know what the heck I want to do with my life, let alone my retirement."

Neither do I. I'm still up on the edge of the roof, looking down at the Doughboy pool. I never had the guts to jump, by the way, but I kind of wish I had.

TWENTY

RETIRED NEW JERSEY SUPREME COURT JUSTICE GARY Stein and his longtime companion, Alice, are on the far side of the net, rackets primed, ready for business. Alison and I are on the other side of the net, not sure we're equipped to handle the speeding projectiles about to come flying at us.

For two gamers in their eighties, our opponents are a force. Alice may not cover as much ground as she once did, but the hand-eye coordination is still sharp, and she strikes the ball well. As for His Honor, he's got an open stance, takes the ball low, and attacks like a boxer throwing uppercuts. If I can hit the ball half as hard as he does when I'm eighty-seven, I'll take it.

Judge Stein lives in Jersey and is on holiday in California, visiting the family of his daughter, Carrie, a friend of mine and the wife of Jim Ricci, my now-retired former colleague. I'd watched the judge officiate at Carrie and Jim's wedding in the front yard of the home she grew up in (with a tennis court on the property), and I knew he was one of those people who don't know how to retire. A couple of days before our big match, we met in Carrie's backyard to talk it over.

Stein grew up in Newark, went to high school in Irvington, and studied law at Duke University. In the 1950s he served in the New Jersey National Guard and met a guy named Tom Kean, who would go on to be elected governor in 1981 and bring Stein with him to Trenton as policy and planning director. In 1984, Stein had just finished playing two sets of tennis with a buddy when he got a call. A New Jersey state trooper was on the line and asked if he had a second to speak to Governor Kean. Sure, said Stein. Kean asked him if his résumé was up to date. An odd question, thought Stein, but the answer was no. Kean asked Stein if he could put one together in a hurry, and Stein asked why. "Because I want to nominate you for the supreme court," said Kean.

Stein happily accepted and served on the state bench for nearly eighteen years. In that time he wrote several hundred opinions on cases that came before the high court. Public school funding, insurance company liability, the death penalty, and many, many more subjects kept the judge busy. "It was a wonderful experience," Stein says, but he knew the job came with a prescribed end date: mandatory retirement at seventy. Generally speaking, mandatory retirement is unlawful in the United States under the Age Discrimination in Employment Act of 1967, as Judge Stein could certainly explain better than I. But there are exceptions in professions deemed to require high levels of physical skill and mental acuity. Airline pilots, for instance, have to retire at sixty-five and air traffic controllers at fifty-six. Several states have mandatory judicial retirements at seventy, and Oregon boots judges off the bench at seventy-five. For the US Supreme Court, however, there is no age limit.

Stein says he didn't object to being forced out. In fact, he actually got a jump on his exit, leaving the bench about nine months early. "My late wife and I had raised five kids, and I thought my years on the court were exhilarating, but they were very demanding. It took a lot of hours out of my weekends and limited my travel and time to spend with the family." But hanging up his robes for the last time didn't mean Stein was headed for the rocking chair. In 2002, the same year he retired from the bench, he joined his son's law firm, and he's still there.

"Moving on for me meant having a career again as a lawyer and helping my son build his law firm," says Stein. "There were seven lawyers when I joined and now it's almost seventy, and we built a firm with a culture that has made it one of the most attractive in the state to work at." Stein essentially works full-time but not overtime, if he can help it. He's built more leisure into his schedule for cycling, running, and tennis, and time with Alice, his five kids, and sixteen grandchildren. As he's explaining his new routines to me, Alice steps in with some perspective.

"You have to understand something," she says. "Gary and I have known one another for over sixty years. His late wife and my late husband died within six months of one another. Every Valentine's Day, the four of us went out to dinner. His wife was my dear, good friend for forty-three years. Gary and I are not married, and in terms of spending time together, he comes every night for dinner at my place and he's there on weekends. He has his life and his work, and I know he has to go to work every day and I do my thing."

It sounds like a perfect arrangement, but I ask Alice if she thinks Gary will ever leave his current job altogether.

"No, never," she says. "His late wife said to me, 'Gary will never retire.' She understood that side of him, that he would always be working."

Stein tells me he can't imagine being retired, and it's not as if he's just clocking hours. He wants to continue using his skills, he says, and be of service, because that's not work, it's life. He does a lot of pro bono legal work, and a particular passion is trying to find ways, through advocacy and the law, to desegregate the public schools in New Jersey. He and some colleagues formed a nonprofit several years ago called the New Jersey Coalition for Diverse and Inclusive Schools, which began strategizing on various remedies. This is an issue that, for Stein, goes back seventy years, to his time as a young student at Duke, as he explained in a 2017 interview for the New Jersey Supreme Court Oral History Program. "When I got to Durham in 1950, I was horrified to learn that blacks had to ride in the back of the bus, that they had separate bathrooms, separate water fountains, that black public school students were bussed to black schools as a matter of North Carolina law. I simply had no idea, until I got there, that that was the situation, and it bothered me very much. I got into trouble many times by riding in the back of public buses going downtown to Durham and having bus drivers holler at me. But it just seemed like just a terrible practice, and I didn't like it."[1]

Stein later realized that segregation was no less pervasive in the North. New Jersey schools, he learned, were among the most racially divided in the country. By 2017, Stein had established a public-interest law center at his son's firm, and in 2018, on the sixty-fourth anniversary of *Brown v. Board of Education*—the landmark US Supreme Court ruling that declared school segregation unconstitutional—Stein and others spearheaded the filing of a lawsuit against the state of New Jersey. The litigation highlights racial and economic disparities and the achievement gap and calls for students to be allowed to attend schools other than those in which minorities are a nearly exclusive majority. This benefits black and Latino students, Stein argues, and it also benefits students at predominantly white schools.

"What I'm doing today is work that I love," Stein tells me.

And he's doing it nearly twenty years into "retirement."

—⁓—

Gary Stein isn't a boomer, but he set a course now followed by millions of people of my generation. What we've been witnessing among boomers, says cultural historian Larry Samuel, "is a rejection of their parents' model of… mandatory retirement at sixty-five, and if you could afford it, you move to a warm place, play golf, socialize, and play with the grandkids." Some people, says Samuel, "don't want to play golf all day. Or they like boats, but they don't want to sit on a boat all day. They want to get up in the morning and live a life with purpose and meaning." Samuel, sixty-four, has a nine-year-old daughter and tells me he intends to keep working indefinitely. He has written several books on aging and says he's often criticized by millennials for defending the ambitions and achievements of boomers, one of which is the obliteration of the concept of retirement as it's known. The old model, Samuel wrote in an article for *Psychology Today*,

> just doesn't have the same appeal for a generation known for an ethos of achievement and for rocking the boat. Instead, most boomers continue to work (assuming they have not been dismissed from Corporate America because of their age), padding their estates that will be left to children and grandchildren.
>
> Is this a good thing? Maybe or maybe not, depending of course on the individual. I'm finding that those who are extending their

second act into their 60s and 70s simply don't know what else to do in their third act, as that is something not taught at Harvard Business School or anywhere else. We are well trained to get and keep jobs, but little if any *attention* is paid to what to do after our careers run their course and to the range of emotions that are attached to *retirement*. So we keep doing what we know how to do, even if we may feel this is probably not the best use of our limited time and energy.[2]

Ken Dychtwald, seventy-one, is still working as a gerontologist, author, and aging consultant, and he is very much on the same wavelength as Samuel. The very idea of modern retirement in the United States was begun in the twentieth century, says Dychtwald, "and was largely initiated because unemployment levels were so high, and we had to get rid of older people to make room for the young. Social Security helped accomplish that." But people are living much longer lives now, says Dychtwald, and in the postindustrial economy, we are much less likely to stick with one job in one industry for our entire working lives. Boomers like us, says Dychtwald, grew up at a time when there were three major television networks and three flavors of ice cream. But the world has been radically altered in our lifetime, and we're much more inclined to want to sample options that were not available to us decades ago.

"I still work, but I don't work as much. I take much more time off, and half my work now is for free. You would call that volunteering or pro bono, but I don't have to call it anything. I don't get paid for all of it, but my work is every bit as nourishing as it was, and what I benefit from is variety. Doing the same thing for forty or fifty years can kind of deaden you," Dychtwald says.

He warns me that there is no clear path and no guarantee of fulfillment for most people who are in this stage of largely experimental transition. But millions of people are about to have "more freedom than they've ever felt in their lives, and they're not used to that" in a nation in which working people take so little vacation, comparatively speaking. So, for some, maybe slowing down will be better than jumping off a speeding locomotive. "How would you feel if you only worked three or four days a week in a phased retirement or a flex retirement?" Dychtwald asks. "Some companies don't want to lose all their talent, and there may be a lot more flexibility and late blooming in the years ahead. We're also going to see more and more people trying out retirement and deciding it's not for them."

As for late bloomers, Dychtwald has a story to tell. His brother is a few years older than he, never been married, has no children. After retirement, he cared for his parents in Florida, but in Dychtwald's mind, would have benefited from adding another pursuit to his daily calendar. "One day I said to him, 'I'll give you something to do.' He said, 'What could I possibly do?' I said, 'You were a great drummer as a kid, and I'm going to sign you up for some drum lessons.'" His brother was skeptical. He told Dychtwald he hadn't played in fifty years. But Dychtwald had a hunch this would work, so he found a drum teacher in Delray Beach. And? "I've never heard my brother so giddy."

Dychtwald says his brother put together a band that's constantly booked. "Most of the gigs he plays are for senior centers or nursing homes, and he loves playing music every day.... So I think late blooming is possible. We just have to be willing to try new things."

—m—

On the list of new things I might throw myself into if I retire, music is near the top. But not drums, because it wouldn't be long before Alison took a match and set fire to my sticks. I know a few guitar chords, but I don't really know my way around the fret board. The piano interests me more than the guitar, but it would probably take years for me to make any progress on keyboards. Also, Alison plays piano, and I am reasonably certain that in my first two or three days of learning to play her piano, which is in the den (a room that also serves as her office), she would slam the keyboard cover down on my fingers.

Health permitting, I'd walk more in retirement than I do now and probably play a little more tennis. Speaking of, in our big showdown, Judge Stein, Alice, Alison, and I outdo ourselves in an evenly played match. On all the close calls, I defer to the judge, because he's a judge. The thing about doubles tennis is that you only do half the work that's required in singles, which is why so many people who love the game are able to keep playing into their sixties, seventies, eighties, and beyond. And when that becomes too challenging, there's always pickleball, which uses a smaller court and is gaining in popularity among people of a certain age. Maybe I'll do that. I'll take up pickleball.

Not Judge Stein, who is sticking with tennis for now, and he wants to make a point about that.

Doubles is a lot of fun, he says. But he still plays singles, he tells me, as if he's laying down a challenge.

TWENTY-ONE

IN NEARLY HALF A CENTURY, I'VE MET AND WRITTEN ABOUT thousands of people. I'd like to think I really got to know some of them, but there's seldom been time to linger with a person or a thought before speeding away like a hit-and-run driver. The irony is that for someone who has tried to understand so many people—by their actions, words, even the look in their eyes—I've never spent much time looking in the mirror. Maybe it's because I'm not inclined toward self-examination or maybe it's because I haven't had the time. But before moving forward with a decision on how to spend the rest of my life, I think it might help to check in with two people I know who are in the business of professional guidance: an analyst and a rabbi.

The analyst asks me not to use his name, and there's an interesting reason for his request: he is considering retirement himself, date undetermined, but he hasn't yet let his colleagues or clients know. That's kind of a lucky break for me, because he's been balancing many of the same pros and cons as I have. For the sake of convenience, I'm going to call him Dr. Bob. I'm not in therapy and haven't been counseled by Dr. Bob before now, but I know him through another therapist, and I know that

Dr. Bob is highly regarded in his profession, both as a therapist and as a teacher of psychologists in training. Dr. Bob tells me the teaching is so fulfilling for him, the thought of letting go is giving him pause.

"I want to be around young people, and I have been for so much of my life. They're alive," says Dr. Bob, who is in his seventies and could, of course, find ways to continue mentoring in retirement. You never master therapy and you're always learning, says Dr. Bob, but you do become a wiser practitioner over time, and it would be a shame to waste all that wisdom. As for the other aspects of his job, which involve administrative duties he doesn't much care for, and seeing clients, which is both a great service and a weighty responsibility, Dr. Bob feels he is finally, after much thought, moving closer to letting go. "It's been a really hard issue, and I've only just started to round the corner, where I feel that my identity won't be lost if I stop practicing," he says.

I can relate to the "hard issue" part, and I ask Dr. Bob what brought him to the point of a breakthrough.

"I just started feeling, about a year ago, that I don't have to be a psychologist in a formal sense," he says. "I just don't have to. And up until that point I took it as gospel that I did. So it may be that there's a point at which it happens or not. And if it does, fine." Dr. Bob says he recently told his wife, "You know, I really think I can give it up, and not because I've really thought it through. It's just a feeling. And I don't know anyone who can give you advice on that last point, because there are very few people in the world in the position you're in. But I think probably that the same thing will work in your case, that gradually you'll feel that you don't have to be 'Steve Lopez.'"

That actually holds some appeal, I tell Dr. Bob. I've always thrived on deadline pressure, but sorting through complicated issues, lining up interviews, and fighting traffic on reporting trips can be draining. And sometimes there's breaking news on a subject I'm asked by my editors to write about, often in a hurry, say half a day or so, even though it's a struggle to figure out whether I've got anything new to say. There's also the pressure of keeping up with the herd. I tell Dr. Bob that it's become a far more crowded stage in the last couple of years, as we've hired more columnists, some of them half my age. I tell him that one of the relatively new hires was asked to write a special feature on page one, serving in effect as the voice of the newspaper. A couple of years ago, I tell Dr. Bob, I would have been likely to get that assignment. So my first reaction at being overlooked this time around was a feeling of resentment, a feeling of being elbowed aside. "If they think they can put me out to pasture," I thought, "they don't know me." But I calmed down so quickly, the turnaround surprised me. I came to the realization that the columnist chosen for the page-one assignment was a smart choice by the editors and better suited for this particular job than I would have been. Plus, I didn't really need the extra work, as I was already juggling several projects. So not getting the call was a bit of a relief. There's still a place for me in the lineup, I'm pretty sure. But I don't have to be the leadoff batter or the cleanup guy. I'm still getting used to how that feels, but I think I can live with it.

Dr. Bob says that, as he hears me out, he's listening to someone in a pretty good situation. I'm not someone who doesn't like what I do for a living. I'm not unhappy at home. I've got friends and loved ones and things I want to do and the ability to do them. I've got my health, so far. And yet here I am struggling to figure things out and going to him for help.

"Maybe the problem is that you think there's a problem," Dr. Bob says. "You may be creating a problem where one doesn't exist, and the problem with all solutions is that they break down very quickly. Good ideas have a very short half-life. You're lucky. You can continue the work you've always loved, and you can do it for as long as you like or not. And you can do other things as well. Love of writing isn't what you're complaining about. It's the nature of the form. After fifty years of having to meet deadlines and feeling the responsibilities you have as a known figure, do you really want to hold on to that forever?"

—⁓—

Dr. Bob makes a good point. I'm at a fork in the road, not sure which way to go. That's not a problem, it's a set of options. But that doesn't mean the right choice is obvious. I know the knowns. I know I can keep doing what I do, either full-time or part-time. I know I can quit altogether and do different kinds of writing, either for pay or just for the fun of it. I know I can probably go back to teaching, which I did for five years at Cal State Los Angeles, and I can find other things to do as well. It's the unknowns that still perplex me. The questions about fulfillment, peace of mind, and how many healthy years I have ahead of me. If I could know I'm going to live to ninety in reasonably good shape, I think I'd work another five years or so. But if ten years of mobility and clarity are all I've got, I'd be more inclined to quit tomorrow. All of this complicates the decision, but in a year of milestones, not the least of which is Caroline's departure, I don't want to waste more time standing at a crossroads. And the more I think about Dr. Bob saying that in his own life he's going with a feeling about retirement rather than thinking it through, the more I think I'd like to do it the other way around.

Knowing what to do, Rabbi Naomi Levy tells me, requires an exploration of my own soul. It's a subject she knows something about as author of, among other books, *Einstein and the Rabbi: Searching for the Soul*,[1] which was inspired by a correspondence between a grieving rabbi and Albert Einstein. Levy is the founder of a Los Angeles congregation called Nashuva, which means "return" in Hebrew, as in returning to "our passion, our dreams, our essential goodness, our love, our souls, and to God," as Levy describes it. Nashuva holds Shabbat services in a Presbyterian church in Los Angeles, and a few years ago, Levy's husband, a journalist named Rob, contacted me with a pitch for a column on one of his wife's congregants.

It's an only-in-L.A. story involving the Oscar ceremony and an after-party in which Frances McDormand, who won the award for best actress, noticed that her Oscar was missing. Levy didn't watch the Oscars or catch the story that night about the man who was arrested for stealing the Oscar, but a member of Nashuva sent her a link to the news clip the next day and Levy practically fell off her chair.

"Oy, Terry," Levy exclaimed.

The man in question was a fixture at Nashuva services, taking his place in the front row and throwing himself into the music and prayer. Terry was arrested and charged with grand theft of an Oscar, despite claiming he thought the statue, left on a table, was a party prop. Levy knew immediately that Terry wasn't a thief; he was playing a role and living out a fantasy. She knew that Terry had been homeless and under the care of a mental health agency and that he fancies himself a Hollywood player—a talk show host, a DJ, a producer. And Terry was pretty good at living in the world he had constructed for himself, routinely making his way past velvet ropes at Hollywood parties and the endless parade of awards banquets. In his own way, he *was* a player, posing for photos with the likes of Beyoncé, Paris Hilton, Jimmy Kimmel, John Travolta, Jennifer Lopez, Halle Berry, and others and immediately posting them to social media. If he knew all those people, he must be somebody, right? Levy set Terry up with an attorney who was also a Nashuva member. She arranged for me to interview Terry in the lawyer's office, thinking if his story was known, the charges might be dropped. I found Terry to be pleasant, harmless, and genuinely hurt by the suggestion he had tried to steal an Oscar. He was hoping to put the case behind him and move on with his life and career at the fringes of fame.

"I know enough about Terry to know that he's got limitations," Levy told me, "and I really do believe his behavior is a reflection of our time, about everybody seeking attention, fame, and pretending that we are who we aren't."

I thought it was a ridiculous waste of time for the district attorney to go after Terry, particularly since he readily handed over the Oscar when he was confronted by security. McDormand got her Oscar back that very evening and seemed unwilling to participate in the prosecution of the man who had a few minutes of fun with it. In the end, all charges were dropped, and Levy's comments about people pretending to be who they aren't have stuck with me. Is there a little bit of Terry in me? In all of us? In my case, am I idealizing retirement, having created a fantasy of myself as a contented old man without a bullhorn, out of view, and out of the mix?

"For some people, not for everyone, but for certain types of people, retirement is overrated," Levy tells me.

That is not a revelation, for sure. I'd heard it from many others in the last few months. But coming from a rabbi I have great respect for, the words carry the weight of authority. It's as if a messenger of God has just given me permission to say the hell with retirement, I'm a workingman and proud of it. The people likely to fantasize about retirement are those who don't enjoy their jobs, says Levy. "But for someone who gets a lot of fulfillment and ego strokes," it's a different calculation. Having a job you enjoy gives your life and your day structure, Levy says. "We should never underestimate the importance of a structured day and the feeling that you're needed."

Levy has a friend whose father, a workingman, had a case of weekend depression. "He was fine all week, but when the weekends came along, he got the blues and would sleep all day. It didn't occur to them that this was a person who was happiest with structure, happiest with work. When he had time off, he couldn't enjoy himself. That wasn't the way he was built."

I find that poor sap frighteningly identifiable. As I said earlier, on my weekends, if I don't have errands to run or something to do in the garden, or if I don't have plans for how the day is going to play out, I get jumpy. The clock doesn't move and the day drags. Then I open the newspaper and a smorgasbord of stories gets me thinking about column possibilities. Just like that, I'm back in the chase, goodbye leisure. Should I make some phone calls or send out some emails and try to line up something to write about when the workweek resumes? Then I look at the column I've just written, which hasn't been printed yet, and start tinkering with it on my computer. I should've done this, should've done that. Let me rewrite this damn thing, or at least toss it around in my head, and there goes the day. This has been my routine for decades, an inability to completely shut down and stop working. But I'm not sure it's because I'm not suited for retirement and the increased idle time it would bring. Maybe I've never been unplugged long enough to know if there's another version of me yearning to be let free.

What I'm trying to answer, Levy tells me, is a soul question. She explained what she means by that in her book on Einstein and the rabbi.

In my many years as a rabbi people have come to me with their life questions: *What should I do with my life? Is this the right person for me? How do I breathe excitement back into my marriage? How do I find my true calling?* I realized pretty early on in my rabbinate that most life questions are actually soul questions. We have a gnawing sense that the life we are living is not the life we are meant to be living. We know there is more to do, more expected from us, more to give and more to feel. And we are right![2]

Levy, of course, can't answer the big questions for me. But she suggests it might not be wise to take on two big life changes at once: retirement and the empty nest. With Caroline away at school, I'll have more time on my hands, and Levy says it might be smart to use it for a trial run on what I think I'd like to do in retirement. She says that if the list includes gardening, learning a language, or raising chickens, I should get started on some of those things to see if it's really what I want to do, rather than see it as an idealized fantasy about retirement. When she was in her thirties, Levy did something like that. She had two young children and wanted to be a good mother and wife and a congregational rabbi as well. But she also wanted to write, and there wasn't enough time in the day. So she stepped away from being a full-time pulpit rabbi.

"I can say it wasn't an easy thing for me. I remember going to synagogue and, at first, it was a relief to be able to take the kids, and I might hang out in the playground with the other moms. But after a couple of years of it, I remember attending high holidays as a congregant and going into the bathroom and weeping. It wasn't that I was jealous of the rabbi colleague who was leading the services. It was that I felt I had something to say and I wasn't saying it, and I really felt like I had abandoned what I was born to do."

That's when Levy established Nashuva, which she constructed as a way to put her back in front of a congregation without full-time rabbinical duties, so she'd have time for all her other passions. My Nashuva, I suppose, could be a similar kind of compromise that works better for me than being wedded full-time to the one thing I've been doing for so long. If I were to instead retire, cold turkey, then open the paper and read someone else's column on a subject near and dear to my heart, I'm not sure I wouldn't end up bawling my eyes out in the bathroom. Why surrender the stage rather than cut back on my performances? A person who is always thinking about and looking for stories is not a person who has gone stale, Levy tells me. As a matter of fact, I tell her, I was just listening to the radio and heard someone being interviewed about an accidental explosion that displaced dozens of families in South Los Angeles, where a fireworks detonation procedure by the police turned disastrous. I tell Levy the first thing I'm going to do after our interview is go find that guy, because I want to know his story. Levy says she thinks I will tell such a story in a way no one else would, because that's my job: to bring a unique perspective to a story I care about.

"I think the question you're asking yourself is, 'What are the contours of my own soul?' 'What is the fabric of "me"?' And when you're looking at retirement, it's important to know what your makeup is and whether you feel fulfilled or not, whether you feel that you're living up to your mystical perspective. Are you living up to why you were put here? Are you living up to your mission? You're a writer, and you were given a gift, and every time you write you're fulfilling that gift, especially when you write about things that matter to you and that matter to other people and help this world. So I don't think you're going to stop writing. I agree with those who have told you that if you're open to having more freedom and not putting in the same amount of time at work, that's a way to give yourself breathing space. But you're in this city, and this city is in your blood."

The rabbi has one more thing to say, and it echoes Dr. Bob's experience in figuring out how to know when it's time.

"People will often ask me, people who are in a bad relationship or a bad marriage, when is it time to go? And my answer is that when it's time to go, you'll know," Levy says.

"You'll know when there's certainty, and you're not ignoring the truth. If we're really being honest with ourselves, when it's time, you'll know. You'll just know."

TWENTY-TWO

I T'S TIME FOR A HAIRCUT, AND I NEED TO SEE A REAL BARBER this time. During the pandemic, I've been cutting my own hair, and the result is proof positive that I have no future in the field. I use professional-grade electric shears, but the blade has dulled since I began using the clippers on Dominic. They say you're not supposed to do that, because a dog's coat is more fluff than hair, and you need animal shears. Alison was horrified when she learned that I gave myself a haircut after using the same cutters on the pooch. I haven't gotten fleas, as far as I know. But I call my pal Lawrence Tolliver, a true pro, who tells me he's got an opening on Monday. I drive to South L.A. because I need a cleanup around the ears, and I know that Lawrence, seventy-seven, will be a good guy to talk to about retirement.

When I moved to Los Angeles twenty years ago, I went to a mayoral debate. It was my baptism in the turbulent waters of L.A. politics, and a Mexican American former state legislator was running against the white son of a former county official. The Latino population in Los Angeles had grown to be larger than the white population, but the white candidate was revered in the black community, and the race was expected to be close. The debate was held in an auditorium at the University of Southern California, and before it began, I asked a young African American businessman if he'd already made up his mind. He told me he was pretty sure about voting for the Mexican American, but he wanted to see him in person first to make sure, because a lot of the older guys at his barbershop told him he was making a big mistake. I knew, of course, that I would have to check out this clip parlor.

Tolliver's Barbershop sits on West Florence Avenue, not far from one of the epicenters of the 1992 riots that followed the Rodney King verdict. On my first visit, a lively conversation ensued, unlike anything I'd ever witnessed. Men of all ages stood up and made their opinions known with dramatic oratories, speaking to and sometimes over each other, with barbs as sharp as Mr. Tolliver's shears. They talked politics, sports, history, culture, race, and more. When one thespian left, another came through the door, just as opinionated as the last. My first time there, Mr. Tolliver told me I was welcome to take a seat and join the conversation or just observe. I didn't have the performance skills these guys had, so I mostly kept my mouth shut, typing away as fast as I could, piling up material for a column. One customer held forth on the mayoral debate, insisting—as the young man at the USC debate had told me—that the white candidate was a sure bet because his father had been a trusted friend of the black community. Maybe, someone shouted, but the father wasn't running for mayor, because he was *dead*.

But the apple doesn't fall far from the tree, one patron said.

Yeah, said another, but you don't go to the supermarket and buy just any apples. You touch them, squeeze them, smell them. You gotta pick the right one.

And so it went, every time I entered Tolliver's shop, a neighborhood institution for half a century. I met ministers, principals, corporate executives, parolees, students, and electrical engineers, and the political perspectives ran from right to left on crime, healthcare, politics, public education, and the right to bear arms. When the 2002 movie *Barbershop* came out, I took several regulars to the Magic Johnson Theaters to see what they thought. Most of the guys found it reasonably enjoyable, but Mr. Tolliver was disappointed. He didn't think the characters or the conversations in the movie did justice to the real thing.

I can't believe how much time has passed. I was in my forties when I first entered Tolliver's. Now I'm sixty-seven and Lawrence is moving up on eighty, though you wouldn't know it looking at him. Five or six regulars are in the shop when I arrive, guys I've seen there many times before. All of them are retirement age, but then, so is Lawrence, who's still on his feet. His lovingly decorated shop is a museum of black history, every wall covered with photos: Nelson Mandela, Dr. Martin Luther King Jr., Malcolm X, Barack Obama. Several of the columns I've written about Tolliver's over the years are framed and share wall space with Lawrence's heroes. For some reason, as I wait for my haircut, I try to imagine what it would be like for Lawrence to dismantle this place. He's in his element here, in this sanctuary he's created. It's a place of business, sure, and I don't underestimate the physical toll of having to be on your feet all day, circling your target. But it's more than that. It's like a clubhouse in here, and most of the customers are longtime friends who rely on Tolliver. Not just as a barber, but as a mate, someone with a shared history and love of Los Angeles. Someone who takes pride in the achievements of African Americans and at the same time is heartbroken by the lingering presence of racial division and the lack of progress so long after the 1992 riots.

Lawrence announces to his customers that I'm writing about retirement, and when they share their thoughts, there's a common thread. They all retired from longtime careers, but they haven't stopped working entirely. For these particular guys, that's mostly by choice rather than necessity. But Rod Wright, a former state legislator working as a consultant and property manager, says he fears the pandemic ended up delaying retirement plans for many people in the black community. In the last year, he says, people with money made money and people living on the edge fell further behind. Many African American people, he says, are still feeling the effects of the gradual collapse of L.A.'s manufacturing and aerospace economies, which offered union wages and pensions. "If I went to, say, a community meeting in this neighborhood and asked people, 'Okay, what's a 401(k)?', a lot of them wouldn't know." Tolliver chimes in to say he had a customer who did well in the aerospace industry but lost everything around the time of the financial crash, including his house and retirement fund. "I let him shine shoes in here to make a little extra money," he says.

Maurice Kitchens did well in the insurance business, but twenty-five long years of fifty- to sixty-hour workweeks took a toll. He said he watched colleagues go down with heart attacks, and the last time he was forced to turn in his annual MBO goals (management by objective), he knew he'd had enough. "My goal was to get the hell out of there," says Kitchens, who had been involved in community theater in Chicago and wanted to throw himself into that world. "I wrote a play that won an NAACP award," says Kitchens, who has gone on to direct, produce, and act, having never let go of the dream. I feel lucky hearing him talk about how unfulfilled he was in his first career and how happy he is now. From the beginning of my career, I've done what I wanted to do, and I'm reminded of Dr. Bob's advice: maybe my problem is not a problem.

William Taylor, who has a college degree in sociology and worked for many years in moving and storage, is still in the same business, but he's scaled it way back. He says he's always had a desire to be a writer, and he's always resented a college teacher who discouraged that dream. He says that when he learned that I was teaching at Cal State Los Angeles, he would love to have enrolled but couldn't fit it into his schedule. It's never too late to take some classes, I tell him, and as I do, I'm thinking about how I need to do something about my own longing to get fluent in at least one or two languages. I'd rather try and not be very good at it than regret not making an honest effort.

Lawrence Walker, who was an executive at IBM and Xerox, has set the bar high for what he hopes to accomplish in his post-corporate life. "I'm developing a program to save the world," he says. Several years ago, Walker created a board game called Earth Encounters, and he tells me he's now developing a digital version. Players draw cards with questions about art, physics, finance, history, and other subjects, and the game includes role-playing prompts. For instance, pretend you're Abraham Lincoln and explain why you signed the Emancipation Proclamation. "We wanted people to have a greater awareness of all the issues you will deal with as . . . a responsible adult on this planet," Walker told *USA Today*, which did a story about his goal of bridging gaps and making the world a better place through education and intelligent conversation.[1]

And my friend Lawrence Tolliver?

"In my personal opinion," he says while cutting a customer's hair, "a retirement would not work for me."

I recall a conversation I had several years ago with Tolliver's wife, Bernadette, about him considering retirement. She said at the time that the shop had become such a vital institution in South Los Angeles, it would be a shame to lose it. In fact, Tolliver's has become a fixture on the political circuit, with candidates stopping by to meet the barber and answer questions from his customers.

"I do feel like I'm doing something worthwhile for the community," Tolliver says.

There was a time in his life, Lawrence once told me, when he didn't trust the police, who were long seen by many in the African American community as an occupying army. But now the photos of recent LAPD chiefs of police who visited Tolliver's hang on the walls of the shop, and Lawrence's son is a policeman. He's created an establishment that is a reflection of his commitment to community, a place where people can discuss, argue, laugh, and find comfort in times of loss. Lawrence presides over the daily production as a benevolent, open-minded moderator who knows how to steer good conversation, and it's no wonder he felt like a captain without a ship during the forced shutdown of businesses at the height of the pandemic.

"I was sitting around the house and got so bored not being able to see my friends and be around other people. It was a real hardship for me. I've never been so depressed in my life, and that was a flavor of what retirement would be like," Tolliver says.

When he was able to reopen, with some precautions in place, Lawrence scaled back on the operation and made some other changes. He went from five days a week to three and stopped taking new walk-in customers, focusing instead on several dozen longtime patrons he considers friends. "The grass is always greener on the other side," he says of the urge many feel to retire. "But when I take the time to analyze the situation, this barbershop is part of my life, and it's been that way for over fifty years." He's in pretty good health but does worry about declining vision. "When I get to the point where I can't give a good haircut, I'll probably retire. But the way it is now, I just wanna hang out with guys I know and cut hair."

I've felt privileged over the years to be welcomed into Lawrence's life, and the stories I've written are a testament to one of the best things about my job. I understand the city better and myself as well through the people I've gotten to know at the barbershop. I walked with Lawrence and his family to their neighborhood polling place when he was able to do something he thought would never be possible in his lifetime: vote for a black presidential candidate. I went to his seventy-fifth birthday party, at which he flopped on the floor and writhed like a man half his age, doing a dance he called the Gator. He came to my sixty-fifth birthday party with Bernadette, and he frequently reminds me he'd be happy to visit my buddy Nathaniel, who lives in a mental institution, and give him a haircut.

Years ago, Lawrence's son, a military veteran who was in the police academy in Houston, battled brain cancer. He'd be fine for a while, then sick again, and this went on for years until his death at the age of thirty-nine. When I heard the news I called to offer my condolences. Lawrence told me his son would be laid to rest in Los Angeles, and he was on his way to the funeral home. I assumed he had to make funeral arrangements, but he said no, that had already been taken care of. He was going to give his son a haircut. I was at his house a few minutes later, and we drove to the mortuary together. I worried that maybe I was imposing, but Lawrence said no, not at all. I knew this would make a powerful and relatable story about a father's love in a time of grief, and I felt honored that Lawrence trusted me to pay proper tribute. In such times, I can't imagine doing anything other than being present in the lives of others as a witness and as a chronicler of life. I do believe we're united by stories, that they help us make sense of a complicated world and of our own hopes and fears.

"That's my boy," Lawrence said when a blue blanket was pulled back to reveal his handsome young son. Lawrence proceeded to grab his barber tools out of a bag and give Lawrence Tolliver III a haircut, just as he had given his own father a haircut before his burial. Lawrence was meticulous as he trimmed his son's hair and beard, working carefully around a scar left by brain surgery. I couldn't imagine the courage it must have taken to remain calm and composed, but to Lawrence, this was a father's last gift to a son. He reminded himself that, after so much pain and suffering, his son was at peace. He told me we are who we are and do what we can in difficult times. This was what Lawrence wanted to do for his son. He wanted him to look his best.

He was a barber.

TWENTY-THREE

THE RUMORS ARE FLYING NOW AMONG MY FELLOW *L.A. Times* journalists. The word is that buyouts may be available for the taking. A buyout is a corporate cost-cutting tool that's been used by auto manufacturers, financial institutions, and numerous other industries to trim payroll costs. Depending on the terms, it can be a heck of a lot better deal for employees than getting a pink slip and an escort to the parking lot. Buyouts are optional, and for people my age who work in the battered news industry, they're hard to turn down. The company essentially pays you to walk away and go play golf or raise goats, whatever you choose to do, and depending on the specifics of the offer, the longer you've worked, the more you get paid to clean out your desk and get lost.

For roughly the first half of my career, newspapers kept growing readership and advertising revenue, piling up huge profits. Throughout the second half of my career, the business has been in free fall, losing readers and advertising dollars as the media landscape became revolutionized and digitalized. It used to be that a newspaper wasn't just where you got your news, it was the place for you to sell a bicycle or a car. But Craigslist put an end to classified advertising. Once upon a time, newspapers were filled with full-page ads from department stores selling pots and pans and lingerie. But department stores have been torpedoed by the likes of Amazon, leaving giant holes in shopping malls and the pages of newspapers. There's more to the story of how newspapers lost their monopoly when digital news outlets and twenty-four-hour cable news flooded the market. But the bottom line is that the decline of my industry has accelerated, with the number of employees dropping by roughly 50 percent between 2008 and 2019, going from about 71,000 staffers nationally to 35,000. It's been a bloodbath, and the slaughter comes in the form of shutdowns, layoffs, and buyouts.

This is not the first time I've seriously considered taking a buyout. I actually put in for one several years ago, but my application was rejected. I was deemed to come under a "specialized" job heading that was not eligible for the cash-and-carry program. I consulted an attorney who told me I wouldn't stand a chance of winning a fight for a buyout, so I began shopping for another job. But just as I went fishing, along came a savior by the name of Patrick Soon-Shiong, a multibillionaire Los Angeles physician who was born in South Africa, made his fortune developing a cancer treatment drug in the United States, and plowed some of those profits into the purchase and rebirth of the *L.A. Times*. It was like a resuscitation from cardiac arrest, and I couldn't believe our luck. But despite our good fortune, struggles continue, and the buyout offer is being dangled as a way for the company to address the stress of pandemic revenue declines and stabilize the operation before moving forward.

There's no guarantee my application would be accepted. The company might have a quota in mind, and there could be a crowd at the exits. But there's no promise that, if I stay, my job security is guaranteed, given the demise of newspapers. And the next time the company wants to cut costs, it might point people to the exits without offering buyouts. I remember thinking, after Dr. Bob told me I was in a good position because, if I wanted to, I could work forever, "Well, Doc, not necessarily." Even though I've got name recognition, given the nature of my particular job and the little mug shot of me that runs in the paper, we are living in an age in which everyone is expendable. With buyout offers, the thing that keeps you up at night is the possibility that this may be the last one to come around, so maybe you better grab it while it's there. The terms of the deal aren't known at the moment, but based on rumor and past offers, my twenty years at the *L.A. Times* could mean that if I take the buyout, I'd get about ten months of pay with benefits. That would take me almost to age sixty-nine, one year away from maximum Social Security benefits and mandatory withdrawals from retirement funds. In other words, it's all very tempting, and I have one more incentive for taking a buyout.

My editor, Sue Horton, is considering a run for the exits.

Sue and I have worked together for about fifteen years. It's not necessarily easy for writers and editors to find good fits, because newsrooms are like rubber rooms, filled with strong personalities and the full range of talent, ego, and insecurity. But Sue and I meshed from the beginning. An odd thing about her—one of them, anyway—is that she fancies herself a doctor. If she hears about anyone experiencing ailments of any type, she's ready with a diagnosis and believes it to be unimpeachable. Like, oh, that's emphysema or that's Lyme disease or that's Asperger's. I wouldn't be surprised to turn on the nightly news and see Sue being escorted out of a hospital in handcuffs, wearing a white lab coat and being placed under arrest for performing surgeries on unsuspecting patients. I mention this only because Sue says that, as both an editor and an imaginary doctor, she honors a solemn oath: do no harm. That means that when someone turns in a story or a column, she wants to make sure not to mangle it. She's being modest when she says that, because she's never mangled anything I've handed over to her. In fact, Dr. Horton has often used her surgical skills to make columns better by sharpening the focus or rearranging the furniture. Many, many times I'll hear from a reader saying, hey, really liked that line you had in today's column, and it's not something I've written myself. Guess who. I like having an editor who's smarter than I am and willing to politely tell me that what I just wrote needs major surgery, which Sue is always happy to perform.

If Sue has already made up her mind about abandoning me and the mission, she's hiding it reasonably well. I've tried to get her to spill the beans. I've tried guilting her too. What kind of person would take a buyout and get paid not to work at a time when the newspaper she claims to love is short on cash? But Sue hates the commute to work, and she would love to never again have to suffer the soul-sucking indignity of L.A.'s daily slow-motion schlep. She says she has not a single worry that her retirement won't be filled with things to do, from writing books to hiking and gardening and cooking and traveling. She says that her mother died at seventy-five, so if she were to run out her string at the same age, that would be tragic because she's got way more than eight years' worth of stuff she wants to do. But in Sue's subconscious, doubts linger.

"I keep having a dream," she told me, "that nobody takes my phone calls."

"It's not a dream," I told her. "I'm not taking your calls after you quit, and I doubt that anybody else will."

One thing Sue and I share is that we're in decent shape financially, but neither of us is rich, and we know shockingly little about money management. What we do know is that we can't predict what will happen in the way of unexpected expenses: a serious illness, a forced stay in a nursing home, a tree crashing through the roof, an earthquake knocking the house off the foundation. But Sue seems more inclined than I am to take the risk, and she has a strong feeling about what she thinks would be a big mistake on my part. She doesn't argue against me either retiring or working until the day I die, but she thinks a hybrid plan in which I scale back my output and take a corresponding pay cut would be a mistake. "You're not going to scale back," she insists. "I know you, and when something is happening, you're going to want to write about it even if you're off duty. So you're going to keep doing the same amount of work and get paid less for it." As her theory goes, something is always going on in the California news cycle, so there I'll be, off the clock for a week or maybe a month but champing at the bit the whole time, and never fully off duty.

I don't know if she's right about that, but I'm with her on traffic being nearly enough of a reason to call it quits. It's even more of a nuisance than getting assaulted, pretty much every day, by readers who are on the attack no matter what you write. I'm routinely called a hack, a jackass, an ignoramus, a sellout, and a fraud, particularly in the era of toxic partisanship and bomb throwing. I've been told to go back to Mexico, go back to Puerto Rico, go to hell, and so on, and I've been singled out as Exhibit A for why newspapers are dying. I'm not complaining here. All of this and more I can handle. But thick skin does not get you through a traffic jam, and the worst thing about my job is trying to get from here to there or just about anywhere. At times, it's possible for me to schedule interviews for when traffic is lighter, but in much of Southern California, you can get stuck going nowhere at any time of the day or night. I'd be a young man again if I could reclaim the years lost to drive time in the endless hunt for good material. When I'm finally back home, I step out of the car in a foul mood, blurry-eyed, back aching, cursing all the bastards who had the temerity to be on the same road I was on, and I'm 100 percent ready to sell everything, move to an island, live in a grass hut, and ride my bike to the beach every day. This little retirement dream of mine begins to fade after a quick check of real estate listings reveals that grass huts start at $1.5 million.

What intrigues me about Sue's contemplating retirement is that I don't know anyone who loves working for the *L.A. Times* more than she does. If you were to meet Sue and listen to her talk about the mission at hand, the newsroom energy, and the constant thrill of making the glue that holds a sprawling and fractured city of a million pieces together, you'd think she's going to hang in long enough to be rolled straight from the office to the morgue. But stress is part of the experience, too, for her and for me, and it doesn't end in the evenings or on weekends, as it once did in the days before online editions. Publishing once a day was work enough, back in the day, but now the deadlines are constant, day and night, as the website is shuffled and updated by the minute. There's pressure to get stories posted as soon as possible, to come up with snappier headlines to generate more traffic, to use all the tools of social media to promote stories, and to search and produce, constantly, news that is so compelling, satisfied online readers will click on the subscription button. It's called a conversion when someone reads a story and is converted from casual visitor to committed subscriber, and in the new metrics of the newspaper survival wars, statistics are circulated as both an indicator of what readers want and as a kind of scoreboard that serves to keep everyone on their toes. I'm reminded of a column I wrote about the basement laundry room of a hotel where an electronic scoreboard kept track of which employees were folding linens the fastest. And, by the way, those grumbling employees referred to the scoreboard as the electronic whip.[1]

As for my business, I understand the need to adapt, push, and hustle, because our very survival depends on it. Long gone are the days when we printed money as well as news, and we were slow to recognize that, in a changing world, we had to learn new tricks and develop smarter strategies. I've always been willing to do whatever it takes to help newspapers survive. I've made radio and television appearances by the hundreds. I've spoken to hundreds of social clubs, professional organizations, and school audiences. I've done video versions of my columns, blogged, tweeted, worked nights and weekends for decades, and always, always, always kept a list on paper, in my computer, and in my head of what's next, what's next, what's next. Feeding a monster that never gets enough to eat.

It keeps you alive and it wears you down.

If Sue grabs the money and makes a run for it, should I follow her out the door?

TWENTY-FOUR

O NE DAY I RECEIVE A COMPLAINT FROM A WOMAN WHO has been worked into a lather by my column. I can't say I'm surprised, because I suggested something I knew would be unpopular. California has legions of teachers, nurses, mechanics, plumbers, truck drivers, and others who are priced out of the crazy housing market. The state also has thousands of people who bought a house for a few hundred thousand dollars and sold several decades later at profits of a million dollars or more. That's due to a combination of zoning laws that restrict new development, and to state and federal policies that make homeownership profitable. I have no problem with the people who played by the rules and made small fortunes on their houses. But why not levy a small equity tax on them when they sell, which would generate billions of dollars and make homeownership possible for people essential to the economy, many of whom now share homes or apartments or commute ridiculous distances to cheaper markets?

"We really are not the bad guys," says the email from my reader, who thought my suggestion was rubbish. She lives in a small town southeast of Los Angeles and tells me that she and her husband are in their seventies, both have health problems, and it's hard enough to get by without my attempt to squeeze cash out of them. She says they both retired years ago—her from a career as an educational aide and him as a utility company manager—but her husband has been forced to go back to work despite being in recovery from surgery for cancer. She says she is not at all opposed to helping those less fortunate, and she even suggests a wealth tax on people far better off than she and her husband. She also points out that other countries have figured out how to build affordable housing for their essential workforces, and we ought to learn from them. But please don't add another tax to their bills, she pleads, because they own a small house, live modestly, and can't afford any more financial burdens.

That is a perfectly reasonable response, and the woman seems so sweet and thoughtful, we exchange messages and then have a long telephone conversation. She says I can tell their story if I don't use their real names or anything else that might identify them. So I'm going to call them Ralph and Alice, an ode to *The Honeymooners*. "We're very concerned about him losing the job, and it took him two years to find it," Alice says of Ralph. "He was looking in all sorts of places for work, and because of his age, it was very difficult to find someone who would hire him." The combination of problems with health and finances has kept them from doing what they really wanted to be doing at this stage of their lives, Alice tells me. And they just got hit with one of those unanticipated costs that knock homeowners off their feet when they're still trying to recover from the last blow.

"We had to cough up fifteen thousand dollars out of our puny little savings account to pay for plumbing repairs," says Alice. She tells me she does her best to manage the house and take care of Ralph, who would certainly not be working if he didn't have to. And she said she's begun to think about jobs she might be able to do, if anyone in the world would hire her at her age. Alice says she likes to write and is pretty good at it, which gives me an idea. I tell her that Caroline and thousands of other high school students have just been through the annual college application process, part of which involves writing essays. Some of them get help from their high school counselors, but others get outside help, and maybe Alice could look into working as a freelance editor or maybe she could hook up with one of the many college assistance outfits. She likes that idea, though she wonders if any student would want guidance from someone in her seventies. She'd like to find something, though, so she can take a bit of pressure off of Ralph.

"I think his biggest wish is that we could get ahead enough to take one more big trip," Alice says. I ask if they have any place in particular in mind. "Gosh, I know we'd like to see Peru, and we've talked about Australia." For the foreseeable future, though, trips like those are out of the question. "He's not frivolous at all when it comes to money," Alice says of her husband. "That's one of the things I really liked about him. He's very frugal, but he does like to travel, and that's the part that really bothers him about working. He doesn't have either the time or the money to travel."

By no means are Ralph and Alice alone. Millions of boomers— she's seventy-two, and he's on the outer edge of that generation at seventy-six—have discovered that having retirement dreams is one thing, but living them is another. I know this because, in my job, I hear routinely from people my age and older who are struggling. They thought they had enough money put away, but the rent keeps going up. They did well as a couple but divorced and had trouble getting by when their incomes were divided. They had to dip into their shrinking nest egg to help out children or grandchildren. They got sick or injured and ate through far more of their savings to pay medical bills than they ever imagined. It goes on and on, and I've written dozens of columns about this over the years. I remember a retired woman in Philadelphia whose house was crumbling, with saggy ceilings, broken appliances, and floorboard holes so big you could see into the basement. I wrote about a woman in Los Angeles who had a financial setback, along with a dispute over her water bill, and was forced to live without running water. For more than a year, she bought five-gallon jugs that she wrestled into her house so that she could bathe, cook, and flush the toilet. I've known retirees who went bankrupt, retirees who got evicted, retirees who lived in vehicles, and every one of these stories opens my eyes to the possibility that any of us could end up in trouble, including me. It's one reason people of my generation are working longer than they wanted to, if they're able to find work at all in an economy that often treats gray hair as a liability. Another big factor in retirement woes is that life expectancy is greater than before, so you might have enough money put away to get you comfortably to eighty or even ninety. But if you hang around much longer than that, you could be living in a van parked at a Costco and taking your meals from the free sample stations in the store.

It's bad enough as we age that the road to the cemetery gets shorter every day, but it's also full of potholes, ditches, and other hazards. You lose your mate, the market crashes, a tornado relocates your house into the next state. And a lot of people either chose not to put retirement money aside while they were working or they couldn't afford to. The result is that, statistically speaking, millions of boomers are headed into retirements they won't be able to afford. Another looming threat is that, with lower birth rates, fewer people are paying into Medicare and Social Security, and future retirees may be forced to deal with scaled-back benefits. The Social Security Administration makes the point quite clearly: "There are currently 2.8 workers for each Social Security beneficiary," but by 2030, when the last boomer turns sixty-five, "there will be 2.3 workers for each beneficiary."[1]

Late in 2020, *Forbes* reported that "approximately 50 percent of Americans have consistently reported that they will struggle, or are currently struggling, with their retirement finances. With approximately 10,000 people turning 65 each day for the next two decades, that represents an avalanche of gray-haired unease."[2]

And in early 2021, the National Institute on Retirement Security found some alarming numbers in a study of people who are still working but nearing retirement:

> The COVID-19 pandemic has impacted many Americans' concerns and plans for retirement. More than half of Americans (51 percent) say that the COVID-19 pandemic has increased concerns about their ability to achieve financial security in retirement. Among Americans who have changed or considered changing when they will retire, 67 percent say that because of COVID-19, they plan to retire later than originally planned. A large swath of Americans is concerned about their economic security in retirement. More than two-thirds of Americans (67 percent) say the nation faces a retirement crisis. More than half (56 percent) are concerned that they won't be able to achieve a financially secure retirement. Some 68 percent say the average worker cannot save enough on their own to guarantee a secure retirement. And 65 percent of current workers say it's likely they

will have to work past retirement age to have enough money to retire.[3]

That brings me back to Ralph and Alice, who ran out of gas on the road to Happy Valley, just short of their destination. After lodging her complaint about my column and explaining their situation, Alice hands the phone over to Ralph, who is just as sweet as his wife, and his kind, relaxed manner belies the misfortune he's encountered. Ralph worked at a utility company for three decades and enjoyed both the job and his colleagues. But after a merger, his employer offered generous retirement packages. He wasn't yet sixty and thought it was too early to begin the next phase of his life. But the deal was tempting, and having lived frugally and eliminated debt, Ralph figured he'd be in good shape for decades, particularly when Social Security kicked in. Ralph took the lump-sum retirement fund option rather than monthly payments, because he wanted to invest and watch his money grow. For several years, the plan worked beautifully, and retirement was just what Ralph and Alice hoped it would be. Ralph had time to volunteer for local charities, and he and Alice, both nature lovers, spent plenty of time hiking and traveling, comfortably keeping up with their bills all the while.

"Then 2008 came along," says Ralph, and the market crash turned his lump sum into a tiny crumb. Ralph lost three-fourths of what he'd stockpiled in his cookie jar and never recovered from the losses. Then his luck got even worse. In 2011, he was diagnosed with cancer that required major surgery and left him scarred and partially disabled. I won't go into the details, out of respect for the privacy Ralph and Alice requested. But out-of-pocket medical expenses only added to their woes, and Alice, meanwhile, was suffering with the lingering effects of a neck injury. She also lived with regrets for having been misled, as she described it, into thinking she'd be better off if she opted for Social Security in retirement rather than a pension. And so, without the investment income they had banked on, Ralph and Alice were bringing in a mere thousand dollars a month, combined, in Social Security. And it just wasn't enough to live on.

It's easy to say from a distance that Ralph and Alice should have done this or should have done that to put themselves on more solid footing headed into retirement, or maybe they should have waited longer before quitting their jobs. But I think it's human nature, for many of us, to think of retirement in terms of best-case scenarios rather than worst-case. If you get it wrong, by virtue of bad planning, bad professional advice, bad luck, or any combination of the three, you could end up doing what Ralph had to do.

"I went over to the community center and talked to somebody, and what I asked was, 'Who would hire me at this age?'" says Ralph, who was seventy at the time and had been searching for work without luck for two years. He was given a list of possibilities that included Disneyland and various big-box discount stores. He filled out the applications and finally got a call from a retailer.

"I was pretty happy to get the job as a cashier, and I thought, 'Well, I've never done any cashiering, but it's probably a good job because you can be a cashier anywhere,'" Ralph tells me. But leaving home five days a week at his age, when he'd rather be with Alice, is no fun, and he doesn't particularly care for the job, which pays just fourteen dollars an hour. "I don't enjoy the interactions with certain people because a lot of them have attitudes. They're just not nice people, is what I've found, which is a shame. Some people are very nice, but there's another group of people who just cannot make anything pleasant."

For a guy who's barely scraping by, there's another thing about the job Ralph finds irksome.

"I know the customers don't need all the stuff they get. It's a tremendous amount of chips and cookies and ice cream, which are not the most healthy things in the world. I don't eat candy, but I do eat ice cream and chips. But not to where I'm buying bags and bags of the stuff. I don't know how they do it and how they spend that much money on it."

One day I pay a visit to Ralph at his store. He's easy enough to find, wearing a brightly colored vest, and he's the oldest employee in the store. Ralph is stationed in the self-checkout area, a job where you have to guard against theft, reset the machines when something beeps or freezes, and answer questions from people who aren't sure how to use the equipment. Ralph also has to keep watch over the sacks. If someone is checking out and needs a bag, he hands one over after making sure they've paid for their items.

I watch with a mixture of emotions. Here's this guy who'd been a midlevel manager for many years, and now he toils at the bottom rung of the economy. He and millions of other people of his generation have had to swallow their pride in retirement and do what it takes to survive. I find Ralph's pluck and humility inspirational. When we speak, during a short break in the stream of customers, Ralph tells me he has to see a doctor soon, because his foot is bothering him. He nods when I suggest it might be related to being on his feet eight hours a day.

I sure don't want to have an experience like Ralph's, leaving a job I enjoy, only to end up having to work at a job I don't. While I'm pretty sure that won't happen, I'm not certain, nor can I be assured of avoiding a life-threatening illness like the one that set Ralph back. So, as I watch him monitor the checkout lines, I can't help but think it might be wise to put in a couple of more years so it's easier to traverse the dips and valleys so many re-tirees encounter. The rabbi told me that when it's time to go, I'll know, but she was speaking of a spiritual state. There is also the financial state to consider, and unfortunately there is no price tag on retirement. You can only guess at what it's going to cost.

"This job is adequate enough to keep us going and even be able to bank some money," Ralph tells me.

I ask how much longer he'd have to work.

"Good question," he says. "I don't know if I'll be able to quit anytime soon."

TWENTY-FIVE

IT HAPPENS OVERNIGHT. YOU WAKE UP AND NOTICE THE AIR is perfumed, and you know the jasmine is in bloom. Then comes an explosion of lavender when the jacaranda trees blossom, and it feels like you're living in a Monet painting. It won't be long before we get an occasional preview of summer, and that means the days before Caroline's departure are dwindling. I'm not ready for that, and I wasn't ready for her childhood to have vanished as quickly as the seasons. Just yesterday, it seems, she dressed as a garbage can for Halloween, and was it the following year that she and two pals trick-or-treated together as ham and eggs and a skillet? If I were granted one wish, I'd do it over again, even if I had to get another colonoscopy, like I did the day Alison told me she was pregnant.

These days, Alison and I have the same conversation over and over.

"Can you believe she's going to be gone in just a few months?" I ask.

"Can you believe how fast the time has gone?" she responds. "When you're in it, you think it's never going to end."

The melancholy bug is not contagious, or if it is, Caroline hasn't caught it. A dreadful senior year of remote learning is coming to a close, making the fast-approaching end of high school a time for a double celebration. She and her friends are giddy as the next phase of their lives approaches, with the pressure of the college selection process behind them and new adventures in front of them. Activities are still somewhat limited because of the pandemic, but they're making the best of it, pranking each other and doing silly things just for the heck of it, like dressing Dominic in gym shorts with a hole cut into them for his tail. A second hole would have been useful, because the poor pup went to lift his leg and wet his pants. One night Caroline and her buddy visit a friend who's on her first shift in a new job at a juice bar, and they walk into the place calling out—for everyone in the shop to hear—that they've brought the pregnancy test she asked for. Another night, the three of them go to a Target and buy matching shorty pajamas to wear in public for the evening for no apparent reason other than pandemic-induced boredom and a need to let loose.

One thing that's kept Caroline busy during the pandemic is that, in addition to working remotely for her school newspaper, she and a couple of friends have been publishing an underground online newspaper in which they spoof their high school culture, with one story raising the possibility that the British accent of the school's headmistress is fake. I'm going to miss having her friends drop by and hearing them giggle and guffaw in Caroline's bedroom. I'm going to miss hearing Caroline weigh in on politics, the highs and lows of pandemic response and woke culture, and whether the contestants on *Jeopardy!* have any friends. As for all the people who told me right before she was born that a child will keep you young, it was true, but now I want to bolt the doors shut, because when she leaves, she takes my fountain of youth with her. In the last tennis match of her high school career, Caroline falls behind 4–1 and seems headed for a disappointing finish to a fabulous four-year run as her team's number-one player. But she digs in, chips away, keeps fighting back, and wins the match with her teammates cheering her on. I'm thrilled that she's closed it out in such dramatic fashion, and I'm grateful I was able to juggle my work schedule and be there to see it. But I can't stop thinking about the fact that it's all over. Everything that happens now is the end of this or the last of that.

I go to the dentist one day and catch up with him about his two daughters, one of whom has just had a baby. He says he and his wife are about to make a visit to Oregon to see the baby, and I ask about his relationship with the son-in-law. He's a good guy, says the dentist. Everyone's happy. I'm thinking this over with sharp utensils in my mouth as the dentist scrapes away at months of pandemic plaque, and it's just occurred to me that when Caroline leaves, she may never live permanently at home, with us, ever again. I mean, of course that's the natural progression, and it's what you hope for. But I've been dwelling so much on her leaving that I hadn't given much thought to the chance of her never coming back. My eyes are watering now and it's not clear whether that's from the excavation going on in my mouth or the realization that, at some point, we're going to have to share our daughter with a complete stranger. And because she's going to college in Ohio, all of this could take place in tornado country, a good two thousand miles from the homestead. Intellectually, I know this is how it goes, but emotionally I'm not ready to let go.

"Do you realize," I say to Alison, "that when Caroline leaves, she might not be coming back?"

Alison believes with unflinching certainty that I am, on occasion, hopeless. She doesn't need to say it. It's in her Adriatic blue eyes, where an "I can't believe I married this guy" sentiment floats in the blue depths. She reminds me that, for at least the next four years, Caroline is likely to be home for holidays and summers, and after that, she might very well settle in California.

"But she might get married," I say. "I don't want to have to share her with someone."

Rather than respond to everything I say, Alison often makes her feelings clear with a cruel trick: she ignores me. But I can usually tell what she's thinking, because I'm brighter than she suspects. She's thinking that when Caroline does leave, I sure as hell better not assume that Alison will want to spend any more time with me than she currently does.

"You better find some friends for yourself," she says.

She and Caroline often double-team me on this point.

"Yeah, Dad," Caroline will say. "You don't have any friends."

I've got plenty of friends, just not as many as Alison. But who does? She has friends from every phase of her life, and if that's not strange enough, how about this: she actually stays in touch with all of them. She might have friends from the nursery at the hospital where she was born, for all I know, because day and night her phone is pinging with check-ins. I'm a pretty well-known columnist for the largest newspaper west of the Hudson River, and my phone seldom rings, unless someone from the copy desk is calling to tell me I spelled a name wrong or had the same adjective in three straight sentences.

"I'm not going to be hanging around and waiting to do things with you all the time," Alison says.

Not a very nice thing to say to someone who already died once and would like to squeeze out a few more good years with his bride before the next big sleep. And by the way, whenever

I bring up my death and resurrection, Alison and Caroline give me the stink eye, as if I'm playing the sympathy card or making the whole thing up. Frankly, I thought Alison and I were making progress in terms of how we've shared space in the house on the days I work from home, with me holed up in the den and her in the kitchen. But I may have been wrong. Alison gets up an hour or so before me every morning, and I always thought it was because she needs less sleep than I do. But it's dawning on me that she gets up to have time without me. How do I know this? Because when I shuffle into the kitchen and ask what she's up to, her response goes something like this: "Same thing as every other day. I got up, I took the dog out, I made the coffee, and now I'm taking care of some business."

Translation: "There's nothing new to report, so either go back to bed or go to the den. And don't forget to close the door behind you."

Sometimes I leave the door open and count the seconds. One... two... three... four... There she is, sliding the pocket door shut, with just the tiniest bit of an extra thud.

Caroline has made clear that she doesn't feel it's her place to cast a vote on whether I should retire, but I get the feeling she is not on the fence about it.

"You two would kill each other," she says.

One day I make the mistake of reminding Alison that the pandemic has been kind of a preview of retirement.

She says, "If this is a preview, I don't want to watch the movie."

—◊—

One of my good friends—and I've got tons of them, believe me—is Nathaniel Ayers. I met him one day in 2005, standing next to a shopping cart in downtown Los Angeles and playing a violin that was missing two strings. I tried to talk to him, but he wasn't interested. All I got out of him was that he played in that particular location because of the Beethoven statue in Pershing Square. "I play here for inspiration," he said. Nathaniel warmed up to me over time. I kept going back to see him and he kept telling me more of his story. He was from Cleveland, his best friend in the world was a music teacher he hadn't seen in thirty years, he made it to the prestigious Juilliard School, where he was the only African American student in the classical music program, and he was trying to get "back on track" and perform "the music of the gods" to the best of his ability. What knocked him off track was a diagnosis of schizophrenia that forced him to leave Juilliard when the possibilities before him were limitless. By the time our paths crossed, he'd been homeless for many years and lived on Skid Row in downtown L.A. One day, after we became regulars at Disney Hall performances by the Los Angeles Philharmonic, he asked if I could get tickets for us to see a performance there by Yo-Yo Ma. I said sure, because at that point, we'd befriended members of the L.A. Phil who would sometimes escort us to our seats. Nathaniel said of Yo-Yo Ma, "I'm curious to see what the youngster looks like." I asked what he meant by that, and he said he hadn't seen him in years. I'd never heard him mention the famous cellist, so I asked where it was that he'd last seen him. Nathaniel said it was when they played together in a Juilliard orchestra. "You played with Yo-Yo Ma?" I asked, flabbergasted. "Yes," he said. "Why didn't you tell me that?" I asked. And Nathaniel replied, "You didn't ask, Mr. Journalist."

I wrote a lot of columns about Nathaniel, as well as a book titled *The Soloist*, which was turned into a DreamWorks movie in which he was played by Jamie Foxx and I was played by Robert Downey Jr.[1] He's taught me the meaning of perseverance and the importance of being faithful to the things you love. At a low point in my career, when the industry seemed utterly doomed, I saw Nathaniel one day and ached for what he had. He was sitting on a milk crate in a tunnel, cars whizzing by, playing the cello with everything he had. His eyes were closed. His head was tilted toward the heavens. Ecstasy. Despite his predicament, he had what all of us are looking for. Passion. Purpose. He lived for music and he remained faithful to what he loved through years of pain and suffering. His dream was shattered, his resolve was not. In music, he told me, you take one note, put it together with another, and keep going until you find your way. Among his many gifts to me was the reminder that I had my own passion and wasn't ready to let go of it, and all these years later, he and I are closer than ever. On my latest visit to the mental health rehabilitation center where he lives, I told Nathaniel I was thinking about retiring, and he cocked his head in disbelief.

"Why would you do that?" he asked. He seemed genuinely troubled by the idea, as if he couldn't visualize a me other than the me he'd always known. For years, he'd introduced me to people as "Mr. Steve Lopez of the Los Angeles Times." He'd written the name of the newspaper on his violin case, his clothing, and his walls.

"I've been at it a long time," I said. "About as long as you've been playing music."

He gave me a furrowed brow, eyes downcast. It was as if he was disappointed in me and at a loss for words.

"How much longer do you think you'll be playing music?" I asked.

"Until I drop," he said without hesitation.

"How much longer do you think I should keep writing?" I asked.

"Until you drop," he said.

—∞—

I've got two stories in the hopper. The first is about some women I met at a residential addiction treatment center. The second is about an ecologist who is sounding an alarm on the death of desert habitats. We've been under attack in my business, referred to as enemies of the people and perpetrators of fake news. The hostility, stirred by wholesale social media distortion and accusation, can bring you down, but the best antidote is to immerse yourself in the boilerplate work of telling stories that advance understanding and shine a light.

As for the women in rehab, I got a pitch from Nora O'Connor, who runs an addiction rehab center in South Central Los Angeles. She had seen a column of mine about a middle-aged man who graduated from Yale, came upon hard times, and ended up homeless and addicted to methamphetamine. O'Connor said she would make her female clients available to me so I could better understand the hows and whys of addiction. She said I would meet women who had been homeless and in prison and who had lost custody of their children because they were deemed unfit to care for them. The kind of women, in other words, who we tend to write off, judge, or maybe even demonize, largely because we don't know their stories or can't relate to them. I took O'Connor up on the offer, and her clients were at a point in their recovery where honest self-examination about their lives—the hardships and the wrong turns—was therapeutic, a kind of reckoning. They wanted to talk about where and who they had been and what they wanted next. The women who sat with me told of being molested as children and bounced through the foster care system. I met women who had been raped as teenagers and adults, who'd suffered beatings, been diagnosed with mental illness, and hustled for street drugs to ease the pain, which only made matters worse. In each case, they were caught in the same cycles of abuse, abandonment, and poverty that had wrecked their mothers' lives. I noticed that one of the women had railroad tracks on her arms and asked her about it.

"I used to cut myself to feel that, instead of the pain I was going through," she said.

Another woman told me her father whipped her with a belt and punched her mother in the mouth, breaking her jaw. She told me that, as an adult, she ended up with a man who mocked her and called her a dummy. "Oh, I hated that word," she said.

This might sound odd, but I felt lucky to have met them all, to have a passport to disappear into the dark places and report back to the outside world. When I got home that day, I began poring over my notes. Some columns are difficult to write. With this one, I knew exactly the point I wanted to make, and the words jumped onto the page: "We generally associate addiction with weakness. But talking to these women, I saw nothing but strength. The strength needed to survive what they went through, and to believe they can break through to something better."[2]

The other story, about the doomed desert environment, grew out of a weekend trip Alison and I were planning. We were headed to the Palm Springs area, and I wanted to know if we might be able to catch one of California's most spectacular shows: the spring wildflower bloom. Thanks to yet another year of drought, I feared the chances weren't good, but the desert is full of microclimates, slot canyons, and hidden springs, so you never know. Unfortunately, a quick search led me to a dreary assessment from a desert ecologist.

"This is a disastrous year for wildflowers," he told the *Desert Sun*. "I haven't seen it this bad in memory."

That got me thinking about what else the ecologist might have to say, so I tracked him down and gave him a call. His name is Jim Cornett, and I told him I'd written about the impact of climate change on California's agriculture, its redwood trees, its forests, and its coastal habitats, including the migration of juvenile great white sharks into northern waters that used to be too cold for them. I asked if he was seeing signs of change in the desert, beyond the wildflower bust. Cornett told me my timing was good, because he was researching a book on the dramatic transformation of an environment he'd been studying for half a century.

Naturally, I invited myself to tag along with him, and he accepted the chance to tell a cautionary tale about what's at stake. Cornett has dozens of study sites at which, for years, he has been monitoring the growth and health of fan palms, ocotillo plants, and Joshua trees, all of which are iconic species that have drawn tourists for decades. At the southern entrance to Joshua Tree National Park, we got out of Cornett's Jeep and booted through the dry, dusty terrain to a grouping of several dozen droopy ocotillo plants. With normal rainfall in this part of the desert—about five inches or so—the ocotillo prosper, sprouting spindly, spiderlike branches with deep green leaf clusters and bright red flowers. Migrating hummingbirds come up from Mexico and feast on the nectar of the ocotillo. But the ocotillo at this location were in sad shape, brittle and lifeless. We came upon an ocotillo with a nest built into the base of it, and Cornett identified it as a desperate attempt by a desert wood rat to escape the heat and survive on precious little moisture. He explained the cascading effect that he has witnessed: no rain means no wildflowers, which means no seeds for birds and rodents to feast on, which means no food for snakes and predatory birds. We later drove to another study site of his where the trees were in worse shape than the ocotillo we had just seen, and Cornett gave me the headline that ran with the column I wrote after visits to several of his study sites: "Imagine No Joshua Trees in Joshua Tree National Park."[3]

Cornett, three years older than I, said that, although he was witness to a depressing phenomenon, he was as engaged in his work as ever, and perhaps even more so, given the heightened significance of the imperiled habitat. He wanted to use scientific observation to make the point that if we don't change our ways when it comes to energy consumption, we are going to continue to witness the death of plant and animal species. I brought up the topic of retirement during our many hours together in the desert landscape around Palm Springs and the Mojave Desert, and Cornett said he had contemporaries who were retired, but he couldn't see the point of it. The question that occurred to him was, "What are you going to do, play golf all day?"

Cornett, like Father Greg Boyle in his tabernacle and like Randall Grahm in his vineyard, said he would continue working for as long as he could, because he couldn't think of a better way to spend his time. After visiting with him and with Nora O'Connor and her clients, I felt as though I had a deeper understanding of the meaning of work, and I felt two steps closer to knowing what I wanted to do.

TWENTY-SIX

PEOPLE LIKE MY FRIEND MORRIE, 106, AND MAY LEE, STILL at her desk in Sacramento at the age of 100, are genetically blessed and miraculously healthy, but they're outliers. In fact, it almost seems silly to make long-term plans, because I don't know how anybody gets through the day in one piece with so many dangers lurking, sometimes just out of view. Tom LaBonge was robustly alive one day and gone the next. For a column on how the pandemic had led to both lighter traffic and more speeding and death, I attended the funeral of a man my age who went for a walk at lunch and was killed by a careening car.

We don't always hear the clock ticking, and we don't know what's around the bend. I keep thinking about my conversation with Alice and my visit with her husband, Ralph, who didn't see cancer coming, and who never imagined that, instead of traveling the world, he'd be working at a checkout stand. One day I got an email from a close friend of mine. Two years into retirement, his memory lapses landed him at a clinic where a brain scan revealed findings of advancing Alzheimer's. "Some days I feel very sorry for myself," he said in an email. "Other times I am fatalistic. But whatever my mood, please know that it's going to be great family and great friends that keep me strong."

I didn't need yet another reminder that we're all just borrowing space and time, with ownership of neither, but I got one when my sister checked in with some bad news. The cancer she thought she had willed into submission had roared back.

Debbie is three years older than I. We were born in the small town where our parents were born. Same hospital, even, and we had a couple of our parents' former teachers when we were in high school. Debbie yearned for adventure after graduation, so she became a flight attendant when air travel was glamorous and exotic, and she saw the world, then worked in an airline sales department for many years. Fifteen years ago, just fifty-five, she was wheeled into surgery at a San Francisco Bay Area hospital. Ovarian cancer is sometimes referred to as the silent killer, because many women don't experience significant symptoms until the disease has advanced to dangerous stages. That's how it was for my sister, but when a large tumor was removed, the surgeon said she was optimistic. The cancer appeared to have been confined to the one area of the abdomen. In the months that followed, Debbie underwent radiation and chemotherapy, and the ordeal was proof that treatment can be as grueling as the disease itself. She isn't one to complain, which made her spirited battle all the more inspirational. But two years after her surgery, she got horrible news: an MRI revealed a brain tumor the size of a golf ball.

Debbie was scared. The whole family was. But she is a woman of great faith, which for her is a source of strength and optimism. The hope was that the surgeon would find a primary, benign tumor rather than a sign that the ovarian cancer had lingered and traveled. But when the doctor emerged from the operating room, she told me the mass she removed had the appearance of a malignant metastasis, and she handed me a printout of an abstract that said average life expectancy in such cases was twenty-two months. "I'm sorry," the surgeon said. The lab results confirmed the doctor's suspicion, but when I took a closer look at the study she had handed me, I realized that "average" life expectancy is just that. Some patients in the study didn't last long at all, but others had lived as long as twenty years. When I shared this range with my sister, the queen of positive thinking, she brightened, confident that she could will herself into the long end of the survival curve. "I'll take the twenty years," she said.

And she may get there. But in the years after the surgery, regular brain scans have showed multiple tiny lesions. When one or more of them grew at a rapid enough pace, my sister would be ordered back for another scan three months later, and on several occasions, they became big enough to require surgery. Thank God the technology was evolving at the time, because instead of the standard whole brain radiation, which kills healthy cells and can result in cognitive loss, new forms of laser surgery pinpointed and zapped the tumors without harming the other cells. Debbie had Gamma Knife surgery. She had CyberKnife surgery. And then she went several years with a head full of tiny lesions that weren't growing, so she believed she had won the fight. By the nature of her cancer's cellular structure, or by force of will or faith, she was a survivor even as so many cancer-stricken women she knew, befriended, and supported lost their lives.

But things were different this time. The latest scan, my sister told me, revealed the presence of the largest, fastest-growing tumor since the first brain surgery. It would have to come out immediately, so she began making all the necessary preparations.

Debbie has been through this so often she had been able to face brain surgery relatively calmly. But she sounded different to me this time and admitted she was exhausted by the relentless grip of a disease over which she had so little control. The combination of the cancer and the life-prolonging treatments had left her with multiple physical ailments she dealt with daily, including digestive problems and severe headaches. One eye was droopy. She had a bout of amnesia. I got nervous, and wondered if she was withholding something from me, when she said she had an appointment with her attorney because she needed to update her will before this next surgery. I told her I would drive north and take her to the hospital, and she insisted I wait and see her when she was well. She said either her son or one of her many close friends would take her to the hospital for what was scheduled to be a twenty-minute outpatient procedure, and then she would recover at home and wait on the surgeon's assessment as well as the results of a full-body scan that would search for cancer in any other part of her body. "If I find out I have cancer anywhere else after this test, then you can come and give me a hug before I go nuts," she said. On the eve of the surgery, she sent me a message that made me regret not being with her. "My nerves and my blood pressure are out of control," she said. "I need to calm down. One more time. Love you brother."

—w—

Our parents faded gradually, as if following the textbook guide on aging. The medicine cabinet and bathroom counter were filled with amber-colored prescription containers and those little compartments with the days of the week on them, so you remember to take your pills. The toilet seat was elevated and rails were added. First came canes and then walkers, forgotten names and dates, weekly runs to doctors of all sorts, incomprehensible insurance quandaries. My father stubbornly refused to accommodate any form of diminishment. He insisted he didn't need help getting out of bed to go to the bathroom, and he tumbled to the floor one night, unable to get back up. My mother couldn't lift him, so she got down next to him, threw a blanket over both of them, and they went to sleep side by side.

Debbie decided to move in. She was divorced, living alone, and unable to work because of her medical condition, so she helped them manage their affairs while nursing them in the little house in which we had been raised. She still had a life of her own, with plenty of friends and with neighbors who would help her and keep an eye on our parents if she needed a break. But she was, essentially, a full-time caretaker for roughly ten years. Our father went first. He'd been ravaged by years of heart ailments and ministrokes. He began waking up in the middle of the night for conversations with imaginary people. He was in hospice care at the end, and we had the conversation so many families have about whether he should be at home or in a facility that offered twenty-four-hour care. But like most people, he knew and we knew he wanted to be at home. Hospice care is usually a good option, but the quality has changed since its origins as a small cottage industry run by nonprofits. Over time, the industry was gobbled up by corporate players operating with virtually no oversight or formal review, and consumers have little information on which to make informed choices about which outfit to choose. These companies are excellent at marketing their services, and many of the nurses and aides are both skilled and saintly. But maximizing profits often means skimping on staff, and in my father's case, as his health rapidly deteriorated, the promised visits by medical staff were few and far between. We complained, which didn't get us anywhere. My sister and mother were the primary care-givers, dabbing a small sponge in water and touching it to his mouth when he could no longer swallow. My father died at home, in his bedroom, with my mother and sister at his side through the final days, hours, and minutes.

My mother never really recovered from the loss. She said, at times, that she was ready to be with her husband. They ar-gued for years, as couples do, and drove each other mad at times, but there was shared history and three kids they loved and supported, along with four grandchildren. Like many chil-dren of the Depression, they lived frugally. My father's parents had come to the United States from Spain and opened a little grocery store. My mother's parents came from Italy and also opened a grocery store just a few blocks away. Neither of my parents went to college, but my father hustled jobs, working as a milk truck driver, a bread truck driver, and a salesman for a wholesale candy and tobacco distributor. My mother took care of the kids and ran the household. And now here she was, five years after my father's death, in a deep state of depression. She'd wake up, refuse to get out of bed, and lie alone in the dark for entire days. Years of heart trouble had left her in a weak-ened state. Her kidneys were failing, along with her memory. Near the end she was rushed to the hospital, and when she was briefly conscious, my sister and I tried to connect with her by telling stories about the family. My mother listened intently, examining both of us as we spoke, and then declared, "I don't know who the hell you guys are."

She was essentially hustled out of the hospital when doc-tors determined she wouldn't get better. We found a bed in a residential home that had been turned into an end-stage facil-ity. For care, we hired a hospice agency that, on paper, seemed better than the one my father had. But the results were even worse this time. My mother arrived at the home, but neither her medication nor her nurse showed up, despite promises. Her sedatives had worn off and she was in excruciating pain, writhing and flailing as Debbie wailed in horror. I called the hospice company and demanded to know what happened, and I was told that the nurse assigned to our mother had encountered an emergency with another patient and was delayed. I told them to send another nurse immediately. It was hours before someone finally came, and we fired the hospice agency the next day. The new agency promptly sent a nurse who regulated our mother's medication, allowing her a measure of comfort and peace in her final hours. And that nurse, bless her, attended our mother's funeral.

There are, of course, no happy endings, but there are good deaths and bad. I've always felt that before I get to the state my parents were in—not recognizing loved ones and not being able to feed themselves or take care of bathroom issues on their own—I would exercise my right to die. I don't want my loved ones to have to suffer along with me through a prolonged final stage, and seeing my parents die the way they did, I became even more certain that I want to leave on my own terms, if it's at all possible.

You learn, when you lose a loved one, to be more grateful for every lucid, waking moment. You tell yourself to make the best possible use of the time you have left. My father certainly lived that way. Both his parents died when they were young, and then he lost a brother to suicide in the days when clinical depression was known only as "the blues." A year later his sister took her own life. These losses made my father all the more eager to appreciate life and celebrate family, and he always moved as if time was running out, always eager to travel, especially if it was a family trip. When he retired from work, he dragged sprinklers around the backyard and walked the dog, trying to stay busy and useful. But something was missing. He had never loved the politics and pressure of his job, but he did love visiting his customers, some of whom he'd known for years. So he worked out a deal in which he went back to work for a day or two each week, and that simple adjustment made him whole again.

—m—

Debbie's brain surgery was a success, more or less. The tumor was zapped, and she went home and began her recovery, which took a few weeks longer than she had expected. She was exhausted and barely able to get out of bed. The doctor told her the medical staff would be keeping an eye on another tumor that was almost big enough to require surgery. The full-body scan, meanwhile, revealed a few abnormalities. "Looks like a large cyst on one kidney, a nodule on the left adrenal gland, and questionable tissue near the thyroid," my sister said as she awaited a chat with the doctor to discuss the meaning of all that. But as it turned out, none of that involved any new cancer.

"Pretty good news, right?" my sister asked.

We had a long talk, and Debbie asked about the book I was working on, because we'd never discussed it in any detail. It's about retirement, I said. About me deciding whether it's time. Even if I were to retire from my current job, Debbie said, she was sure I would keep writing in some form, or maybe work part-time, like our father did. "It's not like it's the end of your career," she said. "You have something you can take to your grave."

An irony I hadn't considered was that, as I began thinking seriously about leaving work, Debbie had been wishing she could return to work. In her last job, she worked for a guy who was a local politician and owned a small winery as well as an energy conservation company that installs window film to keep California's sun-blasted offices and homes cooler.

"I loved that job, and I was like the queen bee," she said.

But her medical problems and her decision to care for our parents kept her from returning to that job. I told her that caring for our parents and volunteering as an inspirational speaker and offering moral support to dozens of cancer patients had been more important than any formal nine-to-five job could have been. In recent years she's been checking on aging neighbors and family friends and delivering food to them. She said she had wanted to go to school again and maybe write, but she wonders if she has enough time left and whether she can find the motivation.

"My life and how I handled the cancer have been beneficial to so many people, but I don't really understand that," Debbie said. "Obviously my story must have been inspirational to others and that's great, but I don't look at it as enough, given what I was capable of."

One reason for her mood was that the wife of a cousin had just died, four days after being diagnosed with cancer.

"I don't know why the Lord wants me here," Debbie said. "But after seven surgeries, I hope I can influence others to be full of hope and purpose."

It's honest work, from which I don't see her ever retiring.

TWENTY-SEVEN

AND JUST LIKE THAT, IT'S ONCE AGAIN FOURTH OF JULY, a sunny day in the low eighties, with scattered bursts of small explosives and a film of smoke across the sky from last night's early celebrations. Much has changed in the last year. L.A.'s obsession with fireworks has not. I'm in my backyard again, in the same chair I sat in a year ago when this quest began.

I couldn't have told you back then whether I would better understand, twelve months later, what work means to me. I could only have guessed at whether I would discover what, for me, constitutes Independence Day. I keep thinking back now on the day I drove home from the Mojave Desert, where I had spent time watching Jim Cornett survey his beloved Joshua trees. I was heading west, flanked by lunar expanses of high desert landscape, with the sharp, snowy peaks of the Sierra range carving the sky in the distance. It was like driving in a dream, with a lone car ahead of me and nothing but mystery on the horizon. My instinct, borrowed perhaps from Cornett, was to blow past all the exits and keep driving.

There was never really an aha! moment. For the first six months of the past year, I tended to think in terms of going all in or all out. I wanted to do something decisive and embrace it. But I was too timid—chicken is probably the more accurate word—to go the route of total reinvention, as much as I envy people who make bold moves. People who drop out. Relocate to other countries. Commit everything to a cause, missionary-style. One problem with such a radical departure would have been that, as a retiree, I would have wanted to get up and go places, but Alison—seven years younger than I—is not yet interested in living the life of a retiree. She loves to travel, but she's got her own life to live and her own work as well. Lately she's been working as a freelance writer for the Cal State Northridge administration, and with Caroline away at school, she'll have more time to pick and choose other jobs, including those that involve medical writing, which she's specialized in for years. She was writing about cancer and HIV treatments before I met her.

I do still worry about staying the course and waiting too long to slow down, but the rabbi made a compelling argument for crafting a compromise. In her case, she left her full-time pulpit job and built her own congregation, allowing her to be all the things she wanted to be—rabbi, wife, mother, writer. It seemed in the end that the obvious choice for me, too, was to keep working, but not as much. Alison was on board and relieved, I'd say, that rather than see me abruptly retire and possibly regret it, I was going to take one small step in that direction and see how it felt. But would my employer let me tear up the contract and write a new one?

"They'll definitely go for it," Alison said.

"I'm not sure," I said. I'm an old-timer, and a new executive editor is coming in to lead the *L.A. Times*. I've never met him, and he might have different people in mind to fill out the columnist roster. Asking to slow down could be suicide.

Sue Horton ultimately endorsed my pullback idea, even though she still insisted I'd end up working the same number of hours as I always had but at reduced pay. I took the idea up the management line and got tacit approval, so I began thinking in terms of how exactly it should work. Should I cut back by a quarter, a third, a half? Would I be able to scatter the off time throughout the year, so I could, say, catch Caroline's tennis matches? My first plan was to switch to a half-time deal, but I feared the pooh-bahs who sign my checks might tell me to just go ahead and shut it down if I intended to be out of commission that much. So, instead, I formally proposed cutting back by one-third, with a corresponding 33 percent pay cut. I don't know what I would have done if they'd said no, but luckily, I didn't have to figure that out. They went for the concept, in theory, but then weeks went by without an affirmative decision. I figured they'd changed their minds or that they were going to encourage me to go ahead and take the buyout. As I waited for an answer, I had bouts of buyer's remorse. What the hell had I just done? I was lucky enough to have one of the best jobs in the fast-dwindling news business, and I'd just asked if I could be relieved from duty four months out of the year. Should I pull back the offer? Was it too late to do so? Why were they stalling on an answer?

An editor told me to relax and sit tight. He said the delay was related to a crush of employee inquiries about the buyout offer that was still on the table, and the human resources department was working through tons of paperwork, letting applicants know exactly how much they'd get paid to leave. "Oh my God," I thought, "a bunch of my colleagues are going to take the money and run. Do they know something I don't know about what's in store for the paper? Should I jump in line behind them?" I was weak in the knees at this point, wondering if I'd done the right thing. With each column I wrote, I thought of ten more I wanted to go after. I felt as though, twenty years into my attempts to capture the essence of the place I write about, I had barely begun to understand it. "Maybe," I thought, "I should ask if I could cut back by 25 percent instead of 33 percent." Working nine months out of the year and being off for three months felt like a good ratio. I could see how it goes and decide whether, a year out, I might want to go down to half-time, then gradually ease into full retirement in subsequent years. While I flailed about, Sue decided to make a clean break. She took the buyout without flinching and would soon depart. I'd no longer be able to rely on my steady guide who had regularly made my work better. It was time to go fishing for a new editor, but the one I had in mind, Steve Clow, was considering the buyout. In the end, he decided to stay put, so I roped him into being my guy. I still worried the company was going to change its mind and say I had to work either full-time or no time at all, but one colleague told me not to worry. The pandemic-related financial shortfalls persisted, and the company would be happy to shed some salary. One night, just before midnight, I got an email from a human resources administrator. Attached was an outline of my new three-quarter-time arrangement. I signed it immediately and sent it back. A solid year of navel gazing had drawn to an end, and I slept well.

Every one of the dozens of people I talked to about retirement in the last year helped me make my decision, and I'm indebted to all of them. To those who retired, those who refused to let go, those who wish they could, and those who wish they hadn't. To Morrie and May. To the Leisure World crowd. To Alison and Caroline. To Mel Brooks and Norman Lear. To

Father Greg Boyle and Randall Grahm, who wanted to know, on that day almost a year ago, how I could find a better way to spend my time than to sip wine in a vineyard midday and get paid to write about the experience. I did not decide, in the end, that I am the work I do—it's but one part of my identity and nowhere near as important as my role as husband, father, and friend. Nor did I decide that the world needs me to keep doing what I do. The world will be just fine when I no longer try to make sense of this or that issue in a mere thousand words or less. Empires will rise and fall without me. The newspaper will survive. Other columnists will fill the need for perspective, compassion, and moral outrage.

What I decided, in the end, is simply that I like what I do and want to keep doing it a while longer, if only at a slower pace. In doing so, I'm falling in with millions of boomers who no longer accept retirement as a binary proposition. Part-time work and part-time play are okay. Flex time is trending. The nature of both work and retirement is evolving, with set schedules and long commutes fading into oblivion. This is driven in part by the tech revolution, which has eliminated millions of jobs through automation. Meanwhile, major employers have left the country, chasing cheap labor to the ends of the earth. We are all adapting and hoping we're not crippled by accident or disaster or financial collapse of the sort that sent Ralph, a happy retiree, back to work at a discount store. Who knows? Maybe I'll change my mind in a year or sooner. Maybe there will be a time when I can no longer do the job or when my presence is no longer wanted. Maybe, with three months of downtime, I'll discover through experimentation that I want to do something else altogether. Millions of boomers have figured this out before me. Millions more will figure it out after me, and I hope some will be aided by the questions I've asked and the answers I've found.

For anyone who is on the fence but leaning toward retirement, Sue Horton has offered a window into the world beyond work. A little more than a week into her new life, she sat down and wrote a short take on how it was going:

Last Friday, after more than 40 years as a journalist, I retired. Just like that. Sort of. I'll still be doing some editing for the paper, and I have a couple of writing projects of my own that I've already started working on. Still, after decades of 60-hour weeks and rarely being completely off duty, I'm signing up for a different kind of life.

When I was in my forties, I announced to my husband that I wasn't going to be one of those people who worked forever. I wanted to retire on the early side, at 63 or 64 maybe.

My mother had waited until 66 to retire from her job as an elementary school principal, and she was a great advertisement for retirement—for two reasons. The first was that she made the most of her new life. She and my father traveled extensively. They entertained constantly. She served on do-good boards and organized volunteer efforts. And then, at 75, she came down with a nasty form of leukemia and died nine months later. She was a poster child for both the joys of retirement and the reasons not to postpone it too long.

But by the time I hit 63, I wasn't talking about early retirement anymore. Trump was in office. Journalism seemed crucial. I had a job I loved, and it felt more important than ever. And there's no place more fun to work than a newsroom, surrounded by people who care intently about their work but also know how to amuse and be amused.

I also realized a lot of my self-identity was tied up in my career. Being a journalist means always having something to talk about at a dinner party. It means being invited to give talks and being taken seriously. It means a whole newsroom full of friends and colleagues. Who would I be without that?

At 64, I said I'd retire on my birthday at 65, but then I took a new job that I committed to keeping for at least two years. I told my son and husband that the new retirement date was January 1, 2021, when I'd be 66. But luckily, they'd quit taking me seriously. I'd probably be working still if it wasn't for a buyout offered at the paper that made leaving highly attractive.

My last day of full-time work was July 30, just before my 67th birthday. That night I had a dream in which I was released from jail after serving a sentence for a crime I hadn't committed.

It was hard not to see being sprung from jail as retirement symbolism. But I found the dream disturbing. Journalism, especially during the Trump years, could be demanding and grueling. It was always challenging and often required long hours, including on weekends. But I had loved it every single day—hadn't I? Was my subconscious trying to tell me something different?

I have now been retired for more than a week. So far, I have cleaned out two closets, cooked a couple of elaborate weeknight dinners for friends, written 25 pages of a novel I've been planning to write for years, helped a friend babysit her grandchildren, baked bread, edited several stories as part of my continuing L.A. Times contract, walked a total of 90,000 steps, and taken the dog to the vet twice. I don't have a to-do list; I have a to-do notebook, and it's filling up.

The truth is, I'm a type A personality, and that didn't change with retirement. Part of me expected retirement to be the way summer vacation was as a kid, a series of endless days, of waking up with the expectation of pleasure, but no clear idea what it would entail. Instead, I wake up wondering how I can possibly cram everything I've got in mind into the day, and I doubt that will change any time soon.

But there are big differences that I'm already loving. I rarely have to be anywhere at a specific time, and if I don't get through my to-do list, it doesn't really matter. I'm not holding up a copy editor or a writer or a page designer. And there have been moments of letting go that hint at more to come.

On Sunday night we had friends over for a dinner that lasted late. We sat outside on a warm evening, eating, drinking wine and talking and talking. Two weeks earlier, a big part of me would have been thinking about the next day—about deadlines, and problem stories, and early meetings. About all the dishes, and what time we'd get to bed, and whether I'd get enough sleep. Now, I was content to let the party play out. It strikes me, that's a good way to approach retirement.

When I first read Sue's words, I was envious. She thought it through, she figured it out, and she was already making good use of her time, throwing herself into things that couldn't fit into her schedule when she was working full-time. Sue later told me she had made an interesting observation about the difference in how male and female friends reacted to her retirement. Male friends, she said, were a bit dumbfounded and wondered what in the world she would do with her time. Female friends were more congratulatory and understanding. Sue thinks it's because women are always multitasking more than men, whether they're working full-time or not. They don't have nearly as much time as men to wonder what to do with themselves.

But what worked for Sue wouldn't work for me right now. I made the right choice, I think, and Alison thinks so too. She knows better than anyone that I'd be lost and more than a little annoying to be around without some manner of foundational structure. She faithfully reads what I write, tells me what she thinks, good or bad, and righteously snaps at me for being pathetic enough to quibble over her critiques. I've loved being around her more, and in the year that marked a quarter of a century of marriage, our relationship still feels fresh, almost like a long first date that I don't want to end. Of course, I'm speaking for myself here, but I think we're solid together and adaptable to change. We're going to have to be, because the biggest trip of our lives together is fast approaching, and it's time to start packing.

TWENTY-EIGHT

THE PLAN IS TO DRIVE IN SHIFTS, TWO OR THREE HOURS each, on our trip from California to Ohio. We are looking at 2,266.9 miles of open road, much of it along the Dust Bowl highway referred to as the "mother road" in Steinbeck's *Grapes of Wrath*.[1] "If you ever plan to motor west, take the highway that is best," Nat King Cole sang. "Get your kicks on Route 66."[2] I like the sentiment, but we are going the wrong way, and I'm not getting any kicks. We are driving our little girl to college. Granville, Ohio, or bust.

The Hyundai Kona is a sturdy little hatchback, and ours is stuffed with the things a young lady packs for life in a dormitory. Pillow, linens, towels, toiletries, tennis gear. The rooftop cargo bin is filled with four seasons' worth of clothing, all of it miniaturized in plastic bags Caroline deflated with the use of a vacuum cleaner hose, shrink-wrapping her entire wardrobe. The destination, on the first day of travel, is the Grand Canyon.

My emotions are decidedly mixed, but Caroline is tired of the wait. She's excited. She's ready. So I don't want to bring the mood down, but I can't help but remind her that all of this could have been avoided if she had chosen instead to go to Occidental College, a ten-minute ride from our house. She frowns, bored by my attempted humor. Even though you know the time is coming, as the last summer of childhood fades away, it's hard to believe that a kid you used to hoist onto your shoulders is now behind the wheel on Interstate 40, zooming farther and farther from home with each minute. We cross the Arizona border and make a stop in Kingman, because the college freshman wants one last In-N-Out burger, sort of her official farewell to California.

My one and only trip to the Grand Canyon was thirty-six years ago, in 1985. My boss, Bill Sunderland, invited me on an eight-day Colorado River rafting trip to celebrate his fiftieth birthday. I remember thinking of that as a brave adventure for a guy that old. I was thirty-one at the time, too young to know that fifty is nothing. And by the way, I trembled at the thought of negotiating the white-water rapids. Two rafters had died that summer, and on our first day in a five-raft caravan, one of the boats flipped, but there were no casualties. The rest of that expedition was exhilarating, one of the best vacations of my life. I tell myself now that I need more experiences like that—total departures from my comfort zone and my normal rhythms and preoccupations. I'll have more time on my hands with three months off each year as a part-timer, so my calendar is opening up. This trip to Ohio is my first vacation since my new schedule began just one month ago. I'm taking two weeks off, and I'll have two and a half months of vacation time ahead of me in the next eleven months.

As we approach our Day One destination, the sky darkens, thunder roars, and lighting flashes in the near distance. I check my phone and see a bulletin about a life-threatening storm, along with a warning to get off the road and take cover. But we keep going, turning north with an eye on the storm, a cluster of roiling black clouds hovering off to our left. I'm driving now, and part of me wants to turn around and head back home to safety, to shelter, to a time when we would always be together. We keep going, though, because we have to, and the farther we go, the more the sky brightens. We've beaten the storm, and my worst fears about visiting the Grand Canyon in summertime are quickly laid to rest. I had expected the entire Flagstaff area to be mobbed, but we pull into a parking lot more than half empty, and we pass maybe two or three dozen people, no more, as we walk to the edge of a chasm formed seventy million years ago. The late-day sun is fading, casting magnificent red hues across the gorge. This masterpiece of space and time seems like the perfect way to start this phase of our lives. It's a cliché, but nature humbles and inspires, it trivializes our doubts and fears, our resistance to change. The planet keeps spinning and a new day is coming.

—∞—

They sell a little bit of everything on Route 40, with road signs barking out the assorted offerings. Furniture, beef jerky, ice cream, moccasins, ammo, fireworks, jewelry, tacos, souvenirs, pies, showers, a car museum, and more fireworks, all under one roof. You figure there must be a gigantic mall coming up, and then you find out everything is rolled into one small gas station shop, with coffee and fried chicken to go. Tempting as it all is, we make a few quick bathroom stops and keep moving until we land in Santa Fe, where we've scheduled a two-night stay as a midpoint break. Alison and I go looking for a coffee shop the morning after we arrive and get into an argument about where it might be, with her headed in one direction and me telling her that makes no sense. So we split up to do our own thing until she texts me to say this is stupid, and she's wondering where I am, which is exactly the text I wanted to send to her, but I was too bullheaded to pull the trigger. I could not have found a better mate and I know that, so I swallow my dumb pride and we meet up again, go get our coffee, and relax together in a beautiful park near the downtown square as if nothing had happened. I think we both know why we were on edge, and nothing more needs to be said.

Our stop in Oklahoma City is a highlight. We stay in a hotel on the edge of downtown that was dropped into an art museum, with exhibits in the halls as you make your way to and from your room. We walk several blocks toward the center of the city and visit the memorial to the 1995 bombing that killed 168 people—an act of terrorism that was unfathomable then and now. The victims had done nothing to invite what visited without warning that day; their loved ones were ambushed as well, sentenced to interminable grief. We are here right now. Together. That's all we can ask.

Back on the road, we travel north and east, through Missouri and up to the Gateway Arch in St. Louis, which is grander than you expect it to be, sitting there like a monument to the genius of simplicity. Caroline and Alison are eager to step into the cramped little cars that curve up to the top of the arch, but I would rather donate a kidney than set foot in that death trap. We're on too tight a schedule for them to wait for the next ride, so we check out the museum instead, which has displays of the design proposals that made it to the final stage of judging before getting bumped into oblivion by the arch. It's like looking at the red- and yellow-ribbon pigs at a state fair—so close to greatness and yet so far away.

It's a seven- or eight-hour drive from St. Louis to the Columbus area. You slice through Illinois and then Indiana, and by now, we're all eager to reach our destination. A heads-up to anyone contemplating a cross-country family trip by car: the vehicle shrinks along the way. You think you have a bit of leg and elbow room in the beginning, but you realize it was all an illusion, and you wonder why your daughter needed to lug so much stuff with her. Maybe this is by design, so the blow is softened when your child steps out of the vehicle and you finally have some breathing room. We're only a few miles from school now, and Caroline is behind the wheel as we approach the finish line. She's wearing a red Denison T-shirt and I'm in the passenger seat, trying to take pictures of her at this epic moment in her life, in all our lives, and what does she do? She keeps sticking her hand in front of the lens. "Oh, come on, Dad. Relax already." And suddenly we're on campus, parking outside her dorm, watching her walk inside to get the key to her room.

And how are Alison and I holding up? We're okay, and that's partly because this drop-off is just a warm-up. Caroline is supposed to unpack and then meet with a few dozen other students who will be leaving the next morning on a three-day freshman orientation hike in the Monongahela National Forest. The idea is for the students to do some bonding and then begin school with a new buddy or two. So we say goodbye, but nobody is crying yet, because it's not really goodbye. Alison and I get back into the car the next day, and now it feels as big as a bus as we drive to central Pennsylvania to spend a few days with Alison's mother. Nancy is eighty-eight, strong, sharp, and fun to be with. There is nothing I like much better than sitting under the trees on the back patio of the house Alison grew up in, joined by her mother, all of us enjoying an evening cocktail. And we'll be doing a lot more of this in the years to come.

—〰—

The day has come. It's time to begin heading west rather than east. Alison and I drive back to Ohio for the freshman induction and the long goodbye. Caroline had been out of touch through her three-day trek, but upon her return to civilization, she checked in to say she had a fabulous time and had already made several good friends. We had picked up a few items for her in Pennsylvania, including a window fan and the essential dorm room mini-fridge. When we get to school, Caroline is glowing. She looks the way people do on their first day of vacation, and as we walk outside her dormitory hall, it looks as though she has already met half the campus. Alison and I had hoped to meet up with her later for dinner, but Caroline tells us she's got a lot of orientation and other activities to tend to, so Alison and I are on our own. We eat at our hotel restaurant, a little disappointed that we didn't get to share this meal with her, but we know we have to get used to that, and we know we're lucky that Caroline isn't sitting in her room crying. Here in Ohio, a new world has opened up to her, a world she is ready to embrace. Not that it's easy for a parent to let go of feeling needed. I keep checking my phone to see if she's texted a question about how to handle this or that new challenge. You want to keep nurturing, but you're no longer on full-time duty.

The next day is Friday, and it's no different from Thursday in the sense that Caroline is unavailable. More orientation, she says. I don't know what the deal is with all this orientation. What can they be talking about for hours on end? Seems to me that all they'd need to say is welcome to campus, here's where you sleep, here's where you eat, don't forget to go to class, and good luck. But there will be no last breakfast, no last lunch with Caroline, because they're being run through the orientation mill all day, and then the freshman induction is in the evening. That's our time slot. Show up, say hello, say goodbye, and go home.

It's a classic Midwestern summer night. Pre-storm cloud formations absorb the light of the setting sun, thunder rumbles in the distance, the air is heavy and warm. The freshmen assemble near the student union building and march to the neatly arranged rows of folding chairs, set across a patch of lawn on a perch looking north to the lush green Welsh Hills. Alison and I crane to the left, the right, the rear. We can't find Caroline. She's got to be somewhere in the crowd of six hundred or seven hundred students, but where? Now I'm wondering if we'll have any time to spend with her after the induction, and the way things have gone, I'm guessing the answer is no.

Right on schedule, the president of the college, Adam Weinberg, welcomes the class of 2025.

"Welcome to Denison," he says. "Welcome to Granville. Welcome to college. You are now Denisonians."

At the close of the ceremony, which is short and sweet, the students are encouraged to open their minds and hearts, find each other and themselves, and make the most of the next four years. Weinberg says, "We'll give our students just a brief moment to say goodbye to their parents, and then we ask our parents to leave."

It now occurs to me that this lack of hospitality is by design. There must be a lot of weak-kneed parents, like me, who don't know when it's time to go. And possibly some students who aren't ready to leave the womb. But the ties have to be snipped, and Weinberg is making that abundantly clear. Go on, parents, get out of here. Get out of the way and set your little darlings free.

We get only a minute to say goodbye to Caroline because, of course, she has to go to an evening orientation. The next day, we see her for one last minute, but she can't really talk, because she's in orientation. In her first few days on campus, she has been in orientation longer than I was in class my entire first semester of college. I'm a little ticked, having expected to spend a bit more uninterrupted time with her, but then a thought occurs. This is *her* Independence Day. I've been wondering for more than a year about my own break from established routine. The what, the when, the how. But today, on a hill in a beautiful pocket of central Ohio, this is Caroline's day of independence. She earned it and she's embracing it, and Alison and I couldn't have asked for more. She's made us proud, and though it's hard to turn and walk away, we know we must.

—m—

Alison and I skip the long road trip and fly back to California, leaving Caroline's car with her on campus. The flight isn't so difficult to handle because we're eager to get home after two weeks on the road. I'm feeling relieved, as we jet across the country, by my decision to cut back but keep working. That fear I had about facing two voids—the empty nest and no job to go to—resonates now. I don't know how long my hybrid plan will work for me or how long it will work for my employer, but at the moment I like what I see in front of me. I have more people to meet, more stories to write, more things to learn. It feels as though the job I started nearly half a century ago hasn't been completed, and to hold onto it for at least a bit longer is a luxury and a privilege. I like work. I like the idea of it as continuing education. I like the way it keeps leading me to new interests, new insights, and new discoveries about myself. I like how time flies, and I enter a trance when I peer into the empty spaces of my computer and then begin scratching at the keyboard. And yet, with all of that, I'll have more free time going forward, so there will be more leisure, more travel, more time with my sons, my mother-in-law, and our daughter.

We take a cab from the airport, climb the stairs of our house, and set the luggage down on the front porch. Alison and I embrace before entering. Then we step inside the house, inside a new era, a new kind of quiet. I'm handling it, though. Everything is okay until we're sitting on the sofa a bit later and Alison hears a car door outside. She brightens, then she catches herself. "I thought that was Caroline."

That's all it takes. She weeps. I weep. I can't speak for a while. But this will pass.

Alison puts her arms around me and we squeeze.

"Welcome to the next chapter," she says.

ACKNOWLEDGMENTS

THIS BOOK BEGAN OVER LUNCH ONE DAY EARLY IN 2020. My longtime friend and agent, David Black, and I were catching up in downtown Los Angeles, sharing updates on work, family, and so on. I told David where I stood with a second draft of a novel I'd been wrestling with, and I mentioned that I was beginning to think quite a bit about retirement from journalism. David listened to my recital of the pros and cons of retirement, a prospect that seemed both exciting and terrifying. We both knew a lot of people sorting through that very issue, and David noted that ten thousand people a day turn sixty-five in the United States. He suggested I think about putting my novel on hold to work on a book about how to figure out what to do with the rest of my life. "It's a book about identity," he said.

I wasn't sure I wanted to walk away from my novel, but my conversation with David that day got me thinking all the more about figuring out what to do in a way that might be useful to others at the same stage of life. This is my way of saying thanks to David, who not only has great ideas about books, but brings a passion to them that's inspiring. He found a home for this book with Andrea Fleck-Nisbet and Matt Baugher at Harper Horizon. My thanks to both of them, and in particular to Matt, who was my editor. Matt helped shape the book and shared David's enthusiasm for this story. Thanks as well to managing editor Meaghan Porter and copy editor Ed Curtis. My thanks as well to all who offered retirement insights and experiences, and in particular, my pen pals at Leisure World Seal Beach, who generously shared enough of their own journeys to help me chart my own.

A special thanks to my wife, Alison, a writer and editor, for her invaluable edit of this book and her support throughout the research and writing process. Thanks as well to Caroline, whose search for her own best path forward coincided with mine, serving as a reminder to trust heart and mind, keep moving, and embrace the unknown.

NOTES

ONE

1. *Lost in America*, directed by Albert Brooks (Los Angeles, CA: Geffen Company, 1985).
2. Robert Louis Stevenson, *An Apology for Idlers and Other Essays*, 3rd ed. (Portland, ME: Thomas B. Mosher, 1916), 20.

THREE

1. Social Security Administration, "Retirement Ready: Fact Sheet for Workers Ages 18–48," Social Security Administration, n.d., https://www.ssa.gov /myaccount/assets/materials/workers-18-48.pdf.
2. Otis Redding, vocalist, "(Sittin' On) the Dock of the Bay," by Otis Redding and Steve Cropper, recorded November 22 and December 7, 1967, track 1 on *The Dock of the Bay*, Volt/Atco, 33 1/3.

FIVE

1. Gregory Boyle, *Tattoos on the Heart: The Power of Boundless Compassion* (New York: Free Press, 2011), 190.
2. Sascha Zubyrd, "Global Warming Could Significantly Alter the US Premium Wine Industry Within 30 Years, Say Stanford Scientists," *Stanford Report*, June 30, 2011, https://news.stanford.edu/news/2011/june/wines-global -warming-063011.html.
3. Steve Lopez, "Fire, Smoke, Heat, Drought—How Climate Change Could Spoil Your Next Glass of California Cabernet," *Los Angeles Times*, September 5, 2020, https://www.latimes.com/california/story/2020-09-05 /lopez-climate-change-wine.

SIX

1. Lars W. Andersen, Mathias J. Holmberg, Katherine M. Berg, Michael W. Donnino, and Asger Granfeldt, "In-Hospital Cardiac Arrest: A Review," *JAMA* 321:12 (March 26, 2019), 1200–1210, doi: 10.1001/jama.2019.1696; Salim S. Verani et al., "Heart Disease and Stroke Statistics—2020 Update: A Report from the American Heart Association," *Circulation* 141:9 (January 29,

2020), https://doi.org/10.1161/CIR.0000000000000757; S. S. Virani et al., on behalf of the American Heart Association Council on Epidemiology and Prevention Statistics Committee and Stroke Statistics Subcommittee, "Heart Disease and Stroke Statistics—2021 Update: A Report from the American Heart Association," *Circulation*, published online ahead of print January 27, 2021, doi: 10.1161/CIR.0000000000000950.

SEVEN

1. Curt Davies and Dameka Williams, "The Grandparent Study 2002 Report," AARP Research, https://www.aarp.org/relationships/grandparenting/info-2002/aresearch-import-481.html.
2. Davies and Williams, "The Grandparent Study 2002 Report," https://www.aarp.org/relationships/grandparenting/info-2002/aresearch-import-481.html.

EIGHT

1. Nancy K. Schlossberg, *Retire Smart, Retire Happy: Finding Your True Path in Life* (Washington, DC: American Psychological Association, 2003).
2. Nancy K. Schlossberg, *Revitalizing Retirement: Reshaping Your Identity, Relationships, and Purpose* (Washington, DC: American Psychological Association, 2009).
3. Nancy K. Schlossberg, *Too Young to Be Old: Love, Learn, Work, and Play as You Age* (Washington, DC: American Psychological Association, 2017).

NINE

1. "See Moses Run," YouTube, July 30, 2018, https://www.youtube.com/watch?v=ak_cH_Az7TQ.
2. Ari Karpel, "A Shtick with a Thousand Lives," *New York Times*, November 12, 2009, https://www.nytimes.com/2009/11/15/arts/television/15karp.html.
3. Maureen Lee Lenker, "Mel Brooks Calls *The Producers* the 'Miracle of My Life,'" *Entertainment Weekly*, December 14, 2017, https://ew.com/movies/2017/12/14/mel-brooks-the-producers-50th-anniversary/.

TEN

1. Tyler Bond, Dan Doonan, and Kelley Kenneally, *Retirement Insecurity, 2021: Americans' Views of Retirement*, National Institute on Retirement Security, February 2021, https://www.nirsonline.org/wp-content/uploads/2021/02/FINAL-Retirement-Insecurity-2021-.pdf.
2. Richard W. Besdine, "An 80-year-old Doctor on Why He Refuses to Retire Anytime Soon—'I Plan to Die in the Office,'" CNBC: Health and Wellness, August 18, 2020, https://www.cnbc.com/2020/08/18/80-year-old-doctor-longevity-expert-why-i-refuse-to-retire-early.html.

TWELVE

1. "U.S. Weight Loss & Diet Control Market Report: Market Reached a Record $78 Billion in 2019, but Suffered a 21% Decline in 2020 Due to COVID-19," Business Wire, March 26, 2021, https://www.businesswire.com/news/home /20210326005126/en/U.S.-Weight-Loss-Diet-Control-Market-Report-2021 -Market-Reached-a-Record-78-Billion-in-2019-but-Suffered-a-21-Decline -in-2020-Due-to-COVID-19–Forecast-to-2025–ResearchAndMarkets.com.
2. Tommy Lasorda Slim Fast Commercial 1990," YouTube, October 1, 2012, https://www.youtube.com/watch?v=NfUE5XPthdM.

THIRTEEN

1. Morrie Markoff, *Keep Breathing: Recollections from a 103-Year-Old* (Morrisville, NC: Lulu Publishing, 2017).

FOURTEEN

1. Richard Feloni, "8 Powerful Life Lessons from 93-Year-Old Norman Lear, One of the Most Influential People in TV History," *Business Insider*, July 7, 2016, https://www.businessinsider.com/norman-lear-life-lessons-2016-7.
2. Norman Lear, "How a River Is a Metaphor for Norman Lear's Spiritual Journey," interview by Oprah Winfrey, *SuperSoul Sunday*, OWN, May 1, 2016, https://www.youtube.com/watch?v=s_f2GWtHibU.
3. Norman Lear, *Even This I Get to Experience* (New York: Penguin, 2014).
4. *CBS Sunday Morning*, "What Makes Norman Lear, at 98, Still Tick?" CBS News, January 10, 2020, https://www.cbsnews.com/video/what-makes -norman-lear-at-98-still-tick/.
5. Jack Hart, *Storycraft: The Complete Guide to Writing Narrative Nonfiction* (Chicago: University of Chicago Press, 2011), 5.
6. Heidi Ewing and Rachel Grady, "Not Dead Yet," op-doc video, *New York Times*, July 5, 2016, https://www.nytimes.com/2016/07/06/opinion/not -dead-yet.html.

SIXTEEN

1. Patty David, "Happiness Grows with Age," *AARP Research*, August 2017, https://www.nytimes.com/2016/07/06/opinion/not-dead-yet.html.

EIGHTEEN

1. "Your Guide to Getting On It with Jardiance," Jardiance, accessed January 21, 2022, https://www.jardiance.com/type-2-diabetes/taking-jardiance/.
2. Bureau of Labor Statistics, "Men Spent 5.5 hours per Day in Leisure Activities, Women 4.9 hours, in 2019," TED: The Economics Daily, July 2, 2020, https://www.bls.gov/opub/ted/2020/men-spent-5-point-5-hours -per-day-in-leisure-activities-women-4-point-9-hours-in-2019.htm.

3. Kristina Klara, Jeanie Kim, and Joseph S. Ross, "Direct-to-Consumer Broadcast Advertisements for Pharmaceuticals: Off-Label Promotion and Adherence to FDA Guidelines," *Journal of General Internal Medicine* 33 (February 26, 2018), 615–58, https://link.springer.com/article/10.1007 /s11606–017–4274–9.
4. Klara, Kim, and Ross, "Direct-to-Consumer Broadcast Advertisements for Pharmaceuticals."

TWENTY

1. Gary Stein, "Chasing the American Dream: A Childhood in Working-Class New Jersey," interview by Shaun Illingworth, New Jersey Supreme Court Oral History Program, April 6, 2017, https://www.njcourts.gov/courts/assets /images/archives/oralhist/steintranscript.pdf?c=3kj.
2. Lawrence R. Samuel, "Should You Retire If You Can Afford To?," *Psychology Today*, August 2, 2021, https://www.psychologytoday.com/us/blog/boomers -30/202108/should-you-retire-if-you-can-afford.

TWENTY-ONE

1. Naomi Levy, *Einstein and the Rabbi: Searching for the Soul* (New York: Flatiron Books, 2017).
2. *Einstein and the Rabbi*, 8.

TWENTY-TWO

1. Jon Ostendorff, "Earth Encounters Game Blasts Off to Change the World," *USA Today*, March 25, 2015, https://www.usatoday.com/story/news/nation /2015/03/25/earth-encounters-board-game/70446252/.

TWENTY-THREE

1. Steve Lopez, "Steve Lopez: Disneyland Workers Answer to 'Electronic Whip,'" *Los Angeles Times*, October 19, 2011, https://www.latimes.com /health/la-xpm-2011-oct-19-la-me-1019-lopez-disney-20111018-story.html.

TWENTY-FOUR

1. Social Security Administration, Fact Sheet, n.d., https://www.ssa.gov /pressoffice/factsheets/basicfact-alt.pdf.
2. Taylor Tepper, "Studies Confirm That Half of American Struggle with Retirement," *Forbes*, October 6, 2020, https://www.forbes.com/sites/advisor /2020/10/06/studies-confirm-that-half-of-americans-struggle-with -retirement/?sh=35942c046f9f.
3. Tyler Bond, Dan Doonan, and Kelley Kenneally, *Retirement Insecurity, 2021: Americans' Views of Retirement*, National Institute on Retirement Security,

February 2021, https://www.nirsonline.org/wp-content/uploads/2021/02/FINAL-Retirement-Insecurity-2021-.pdf.

TWENTY-FIVE

1. Steve Lopez, *The Soloist: A Lost Dream, an Unlikely Friendship, and the Redemptive Power of Music* (New York: Putnam's Sons, 2008); *The Soloist*, directed by Joe Wright (Hollywood, CA: Paramount Pictures, 2009).
2. Steve Lopez, "Homeless and Addicted, They Hit Bottom. Now They're on the Verge of Breaking Free," *Los Angeles Times*, May 1, 2021, https://www.latimes.com/california/story/2021-05-01/homelessness-addiction-treatment-program.
3. Steve Lopez, "Imagine No Joshua Trees in Joshua Tree National Park," *Los Angeles Times*, June 4, 2021, https://www.latimes.com/california/story/2021-06-04/joshua-trees-climate-change-desert-jim-cornett.

TWENTY-EIGHT

1. John Steinbeck, *The Grapes of Wrath* (1939; repr., New York: Viking, 1989), 160.
2. Nat King Cole (vocalist), "(Get Your Kicks on) Route 66," by Bobby Troup, recorded 1946, Capitol Records.

ABOUT THE AUTHOR

STEVE LOPEZ is a California native and Los Angeles resident. He began his journalism career in 1975 and has worked for the *Los Angeles Times, Philadelphia Inquirer, San Jose Mercury News, Oakland Tribune,* and *Time* magazine. He is a four-time Pulitzer Prize finalist for commentary and winner of the Mike Royko, Ernie Pyle, and H.L. Mencken awards for column writing. His books include the *New York Times* bestselling book *The Soloist,* winner of the Pen USA Award for literary nonfiction and the subject of a DreamWorks movie by the same name. His three novels are *Third and Indiana, The Sunday Macaroni Club,* and *In the Clear.* His column collections are *Land of Giants: Where No Good Deed Goes Unpunished* and *Dreams and Schemes.*